I0020566

GameMaker Programming By Example

Master the development of 2D games by learning to use the powerful GameMaker Language and tools provided by the GameMaker: Studio workspace and engine!

Brian Christian

Steven Isaacs

PUBLISHING

BIRMINGHAM - MUMBAI

GameMaker Programming By Example

First published: December 2015

Production reference: 1161215

Published by Packt Publishing Ltd.
Livery Place
35 Livery Street
Birmingham B3 2PB, UK.

ISBN 978-1-78588-796-3

www.packtpub.com

Cover image by Brian Christian and Steven Isaacs (Isaacs-sisaacs@bernardsboe.com)

Credits

Authors
Brian Christian
Steven Isaacs

Reviewer
Genevieve Ditangan

Commissioning Editor
Swapnil Khedkar

Acquisition Editor
Vinay Argekar

Content Development Editor
Anish Dhurat

Technical Editor
Tanmayee Patil

Copy Editor
Merilyn Pereira

Project Coordinator
Harshal Ved

Proofreader
Safis Editing

Indexer
Tejal Soni

Production Coordinator
Aparna Bhagat

Cover Work
Aparna Bhagat

About the Authors

Brian Christian is a high school student with years of experience in programming, much of it focused on game development using GameMaker: Studio via self-teaching the GameMaker Language. He has also worked in C++ and JavaScript programming along with some web development. Additionally, he is knowledgeable in topics such as data formats and interpretation, compilers and interpreters, and networking. Other languages he has used include Intel x86 assembly, Lua, Ruby, and Python.

Brian's spark for computer programming began with an online Ruby course from Codecademy. Since then, he has been fascinated with how computers and the different programming languages worked. Since he wanted to know about this, he taught himself C from the second edition of *The C Programming Language* book, followed by the more advanced C++ language.

Wanting to try his hand at making advanced games with a language predominantly intended for it, Brian became invested in the GameMaker Language since he'd already been using the drag and drop functionality, but found it limiting. He spent a lot of time learning how different parts of the language worked and how to use them.

First and foremost, my gratitude goes to Mr. Steven Isaacs, who is a great mentor, and without whom, I wouldn't have this opportunity. I'd like to thank my father and friends, who have inspired me to pursue computer science. Furthermore, I thank my mother for her support and all that she has done for me. I would especially like to thank my teachers and support staff, for, without them, and all the effort they put into my education, I would not be where I am today.

Steven Isaacs has been fascinated with technology since the days of his Apple II Plus computer and 300 baud modem. Tinkering, playing MUDs, MOOs, and visiting BBSs occupied much of his free time. In high school, Steven took a programming course in BASIC and created an adventure game as his final project. Many hours were spent in and outside of school working on this game, and it became somewhat of an obsession. It has become abundantly clear that these activities were incredibly influential in the evolution of his professional life. Steven has been teaching since 1992. In addition to teaching, Steven and his wife Cathy Cheo-Isaacs owned Liberty Corner Computing (LCC), a computer training and gaming center with Paul and Sarah Tarantiles. LCC provided innovative summer camps and after school programs offering young people an opportunity to use technology in creative ways. Courses included programming, website design, graphic design and animation, and game development.

Soon after opening LCC, Steven was hired to bring his innovative ideas to William Annin Middle School in Basking Ridge, NJ. At William Annin, Steven taught a number of computer-related courses. His passion for teaching students to create their own games led to an after school club in game design, then a unit in the Gifted and Talented Program. The success of these programs led Steven to develop a full semester 8th grade class in game design and development, and later, a six-week exploratory course in game design and digital storytelling, which is taken by all seventh graders.

In addition, Steven developed and also teaches an online course in game development with GameMaker for The Virtual High School (http://thevhscollaborative.org/). In his teaching, Steven strives to create an environment that empowers student learning through choice in their learning path. He prefers to think of himself as a co-learner and guide for his students. Steven's passion for learning is obvious to his students as he is constantly looking at creative ways to solve problems, dabbling with new game development and programming environments, and learning how to play and manage Minecraft servers from his students. Students in Steven's class have many opportunities to explore topics in greater depth independently. The collaboration here with Brian came from his choice to delve deep into the GameMaker Language to further his learning.

Recently, Steven wrote a chapter for the book, *Teacher Pioneers: Visions from the Edge of the Map*, edited by Caro Williams-Pierce on applying the iterative design process to teaching game design and development. In addition, Steven was an editor on *TeacherCraft: How Teachers Learn to Use MineCraft in Their Classrooms* by Seann Dikkers.

I would like to thank my students for the continual inspiration I get from them and the excitement that comes with every new day and new learning experience in class. I feel quite fortunate to be in a position where I can learn with and from my students and this approach keeps the learning fresh. A huge thank you goes to Brian Christian for taking the lead in learning GML, which led to our working on this book together. Brian truly took charge and created an opportunity to work together. To write and publish a book with a student has been one of the highlights of my career. It is also important for me to acknowledge my "tribe", primarily, my game-based learning network of friends. We have developed a tremendous community of practice based on passion-driven teaching and learning, something I am very excited about. Marianne Malmstrom deserves a special shout out for pushing me to follow the learning and let go of the need to be the expert. She has taught me so much about the importance of empowering students by watching her lead by example. I have been inspired by numerous other educators including Paul Darvasi, John Fallon, Zack Gilbert, Peggy Sheehy, Matthew Farber, Lucas Gillispie, Seann Dikkers, and the list really goes on and on. Last, but certainly not least, I am entirely grateful to my family for their continual support and encouragement. My wife, Cathy Cheo-Isaacs has become my biggest cheerleader and supporter, truly my partner in geekdom. My mother and father, Nancy and Ed Isaacs have always celebrated my accomplishments and shared in the excitement of every opportunity that comes my way. And of course, my kids, Grace and Leila, remind me of the important things in life and keep me grounded!

About the Reviewer

Genevieve Ditangan, also known as Gen or GenDi, started off enjoying games at a young age. With the passion of creating art and the hobby of exploring worlds through video games, there was no doubt that she would dedicate her life to be a game designer. Although she started out as an artist first, GenDi has created artworks that have been sold at several conventions. Furthering on to dream to be a game designer and one day create a visually artistic game. GenDi attended The Art Institute of Vancouver, graduating in 2015 with her game art and design diploma. GenDi also previously graduated in 2013 from British Columbia Institute of Technology with her Graphic Design Associate Certificate. The road is tough and long, but the passion never goes away.

I would like thank my loving and supportive husband, for helping me through the hardships because without him, I wouldn't have made it through school to carry on my passion for video games, art, and living to the fullest.

www.PacktPub.com

Support files, eBooks, discount offers, and more

For support files and downloads related to your book, please visit www.PacktPub.com.

Did you know that Packt offers eBook versions of every book published, with PDF and ePub files available? You can upgrade to the eBook version at www.PacktPub.com and as a print book customer, you are entitled to a discount on the eBook copy. Get in touch with us at service@packtpub.com for more details.

At www.PacktPub.com, you can also read a collection of free technical articles, sign up for a range of free newsletters and receive exclusive discounts and offers on Packt books and eBooks.

https://www2.packtpub.com/books/subscription/packtlib

Do you need instant solutions to your IT questions? PacktLib is Packt's online digital book library. Here, you can search, access, and read Packt's entire library of books.

Why subscribe?

- Fully searchable across every book published by Packt
- Copy and paste, print, and bookmark content
- On demand and accessible via a web browser

Free access for Packt account holders

If you have an account with Packt at www.PacktPub.com, you can use this to access PacktLib today and view 9 entirely free books. Simply use your login credentials for immediate access.

Table of Contents

Preface   v

Chapter 1: Introduction to GameMaker: Studio   1

Choosing your version   3
The GameMaker: Studio interface   4
  GameMaker: Studio documentation   6
An example project   6
  Naming convention – resource prefixes   6
  Drawing the sprite   8
  Creating an object   10
  Coordinate planes in GameMaker   12
  Creating a room   13
  Testing your game   14
Summary   16
  Review questions   16
  Quick drills   16

Chapter 2: Your First Game – Escape the Dungeon   19

Creating your Escape the Dungeon game   19
  The playable character   20
    The sprite   20
    The object   23
  Walls   26
  Enemies   28
    Making your enemies move   28
    Damaging the player   30
  Making the player and enemies shoot   34
    Making the player shoot   34
    Making the enemies shoot   36

More resources	38
Backgrounds	38
Sounds	39
Keys and locks and advancing to the next room	40
Summary	**41**
Review questions	42
Quick drills	42
Chapter 3: Introducing the GameMaker Language	**45**
Remaking Escape the Dungeon in the GML	**46**
Remaking the sprites	46
Remaking the player object	49
Understanding the four events	49
Starting to code your player object	51
Coding the enemies	58
Random seeds	62
Health and lives system	64
Displaying health and lives	66
Invincibility	69
Shooting	71
Sounds	73
Keys and locks	74
Scripts	74
Summary	**75**
Review questions	75
Quick drills	76
Chapter 4: Fun with Infinity and Gravity – An Endless Platformer	**77**
Creating an endless platformer	**77**
Bouncing and movement	78
Death and enemies	81
Random spawning	83
2D arrays	84
Menus and textboxes	90
Menus	90
Textboxes	95
Summary	**98**
Review questions	98
Quick drills	98
Chapter 5: Saving and Loading Data	**101**
Putting in a scoring system	**101**
Saving and loading a highscore	104
INI file encryption	107

Customizable controls	**109**
Saving control configurations	114
Summary	**114**
Review questions	115
Quick drills	115
Chapter 6: A Multiplayer Sidescrolling Platformer	**117**
Sprite animation	**117**
Spritesheet importing	119
Programming the movement	120
Making your scrolling platformer scroll	**123**
Client/server multiplayer networking	**126**
Networking terminology	126
Printing the server's IP address and port on a screen	127
Creating the actual server	130
Our Asynchronous Networking event	132
The client in your client/server system	137
Integrating Xbox gamepad support	**142**
Legacy gamepad support	143
Modern gamepad support	145
Summary	**146**
Review questions	146
Quick drills	147
Chapter 7: Programming a Scrolling Shooter	**149**
Creating the main ship	**149**
Creating the enemies	**151**
Parenting in objects	151
Random enemy spawning	156
Programming a Boss AI	**157**
Particles	**161**
Summary	**166**
Review questions	166
Quick drills	167
Chapter 8: Introducing the GameMaker: Studio Physics Engine	**169**
A physics game	**169**
The physics engine in a regular game	**173**
Summary	**174**
Review questions	174
Quick drills	175

Chapter 9: Wrapping Up   177

Debugging   177
Compile-time errors   178
Runtime errors   179
The GameMaker: Studio debugger   180
Debugging functions   181

Helpful information on GameMaker   183
Quirks of the GameMaker Language   183
Unexplained resources   184
Export modules   184

Summary   185
Review questions   185
Quick drills   186

Index   187

Preface

GameMaker: Studio is a game development engine that is easy to learn, yet robust enough to use to create commercial games. Budding developers can use the drag and drop approach to coding or the built-in programming language, Game Maker Language (GML), which will be featured in this book.

What this book covers

Chapter 1, Introduction to GameMaker: Studio, introduces you to the GameMaker interface and the basic concepts related to getting started with GameMaker.

Chapter 2, Your First Game – Escape the Dungeon, gets you oriented with GameMaker and uses the drag and drop approach to create your first game, a maze/adventure game.

Chapter 3, Introducing the GameMaker Language, introduces the GameMaker Language conceptually and then goes through a step-by-step recreation of the Escape the Dungeon game written entirely with code.

Chapter 4, Fun with Infinity and Gravity – An Endless Platformer, guides you through the creation of an endless platform game. Through the process, you will work with gravity, speed, random spawning, and further explore collision events.

Chapter 5, Saving and Loading Data, expands the functionality of your game by programming GameMaker to save and load data. The chapter will cover saving and loading high score data as well as a custom player keyboard binding configuration.

Chapter 6, A Multiplayer Sidescrolling Platformer, expands upon the platform game by adding multiplayer, animation, and Xbox Controller support. You will learn about client/server networking to drastically expand upon the possibilities of what can be accomplished with GameMaker.

Chapter 7, Programming a Scrolling Shooter, covers scrolling shooters, such as Xevious, which represent a classic genre in gaming. This chapter will guide you through the process of coding your own shooter, including a scrolling background and random obstacles to avoid and enemies to shoot down!

Chapter 8, Introducing the GameMaker: Studio Physics Engine, introduces the built-in GameMaker physics engine, which allows you to create physics-based games. In this chapter, you will program two small game environments based on the physics engine.

Chapter 9, Wrapping Up, addresses error checking and debugging. You will learn about the built-in GameMaker debugging features and strategies to troubleshoot your code and fix errors.

What you need for this book

For this book, the system requirements are as follows:

- Windows XP or above (GameMaker: Studio requires a Windows-based computer)
- 512 MB RAM
- 128 MB graphics
- Screen resolution of 1024x600
- Internet connection for some features
- GameMaker: Studio Standard (free) version:

  `http://www.yoyogames.com/studio/download`

Who this book is for

If you have some basic programming experience of JavaScript or any other C-like languages, then this book will be great for you. No experience beyond that is assumed. If you have no game development experience and are looking for a hobby, are an experienced game developer looking to master some advanced features, or fit anywhere in that spectrum, then you will find GameMaker: Studio and this book to be very useful in helping you create exciting games.

Conventions

In this book, you will find a number of text styles that distinguish between different kinds of information. Here are some examples of these styles and an explanation of their meaning.

Code words in text, database table names, folder names, filenames, file extensions, pathnames, dummy URLs, user input, and Twitter handles are shown as follows: "Play around with some of the other actions on your `obj_square` to make it do more rather than be displayed and print text."

A block of code is set as follows:

```
if (keyboard_check_pressed(vk_up) && !binding) {
        if (choice <= 0) choice = 2;
        else --choice;
}
```

New terms and **important words** are shown in bold. Words that you see on the screen, for example, in menus or dialog boxes, appear in the text like this: "At the bottom of the resource tree are the **Game Information** and **Global Game Settings** options."

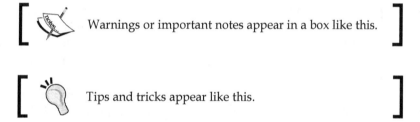

Warnings or important notes appear in a box like this.

Tips and tricks appear like this.

Reader feedback

Feedback from our readers is always welcome. Let us know what you think about this book—what you liked or disliked. Reader feedback is important for us as it helps us develop titles that you will really get the most out of.

To send us general feedback, simply e-mail `feedback@packtpub.com`, and mention the book's title in the subject of your message.

If there is a topic that you have expertise in and you are interested in either writing or contributing to a book, see our author guide at `www.packtpub.com/authors`.

Customer support

Now that you are the proud owner of a Packt book, we have a number of things to help you to get the most from your purchase.

Downloading the example code

You can download the example code files from your account at `http://www.packtpub.com` for all the Packt Publishing books you have purchased. If you purchased this book elsewhere, you can visit `http://www.packtpub.com/support` and register to have the files e-mailed directly to you.

Downloading the color images of this book

We also provide you with a PDF file that has color images of the screenshots/diagrams used in this book. The color images will help you better understand the changes in the output. You can download this file from `https://www.packtpub.com/sites/default/files/downloads/B04888_7963OT_Graphics.pdf`.

Errata

Although we have taken every care to ensure the accuracy of our content, mistakes do happen. If you find a mistake in one of our books — maybe a mistake in the text or the code — we would be grateful if you could report this to us. By doing so, you can save other readers from frustration and help us improve subsequent versions of this book. If you find any errata, please report them by visiting `http://www.packtpub.com/submit-errata`, selecting your book, clicking on the **Errata Submission Form** link, and entering the details of your errata. Once your errata are verified, your submission will be accepted and the errata will be uploaded to our website or added to any list of existing errata under the Errata section of that title.

To view the previously submitted errata, go to `https://www.packtpub.com/books/content/support` and enter the name of the book in the search field. The required information will appear under the **Errata** section.

Piracy

Piracy of copyrighted material on the Internet is an ongoing problem across all media. At Packt, we take the protection of our copyright and licenses very seriously. If you come across any illegal copies of our works in any form on the Internet, please provide us with the location address or website name immediately so that we can pursue a remedy.

Please contact us at `copyright@packtpub.com` with a link to the suspected pirated material.

We appreciate your help in protecting our authors and our ability to bring you valuable content.

Questions

If you have a problem with any aspect of this book, you can contact us at `questions@packtpub.com`, and we will do our best to address the problem.

1
Introduction to GameMaker: Studio

In the 15 years of GameMaker experience between us, we have both found it to be one of the best tools for teaching design as well as the introduction to computer science principles. The drag and drop interface lends beautifully to the understanding of computer science concepts related to object-oriented programming including sequencing, loops, conditional statements, variables, among others. Moving from the drag and drop approach to coding in **GameMaker Language** (**GML**) is logical and the transition demystifies coding. It is also important to point out the importance of iterative design and debugging that people learning game development with GameMaker will become overly familiar with through the process.

By definition, a game is a special kind of program that is run inside a loop that repeats as long as the user has not decided to close the game program. This loop contains code that creates objects that each have their own loops to control animation, movement, actions, and logic statements based on various aspects of what is occurring in the game. The objects are run until the time they are removed from the program. The main loop also contains logic statements that run code based on different possible user input values. An example of such logic would test if the user has pressed the spacebar, and if so, the game will modify variables of the player object so that it rises, and then falls at a certain point. In order for the player to understand what they have done in their game, the main loop contains code to push graphics to the screen and audio to the speakers, both of which are affected by what different game objects are doing.

There are many different ways to create games. Some people choose to write them in native C++ code without any sort of specialized **Integrated Development Environment (IDE)**. However, **GameMaker: Studio** is a collection of tools contained in an IDE that make the game creation process much easier, by providing various tools and code functions that are specialized for creating games. For example, there is a visual object editor so that the developer doesn't have to define every single property of objects in code, but rather they can select various boxes that define object properties. Objects control nearly every aspect of a GameMaker game. Rather than using an external spritesheet file containing separate frames of animation, GameMaker contains a sprite editor where each sprite in itself is a special type of object that contains the images. All the developer has to do is to set the sprite of an object to the main sprite, which will then provide access to all of the images inside this sprite. The main game loop is run in rooms, where all of the objects are placed, in turn creating the full game. At compile time, everything produced in the project is converted into C++ code, then compiled, so in the end, the developer has essentially written their game in C++, but by using a much easier method.

We will begin with an overview of the different versions of GameMaker: Studio that are available for download. This will be followed by a guide to the **User Interface (UI)** of the IDE to orientate you to working in the GameMaker environment. In this simple example, you will learn about creating resources (various kinds of assets) and their purposes, naming conventions, and some drag and drop coding among other skills. The IDE is essentially a collection of integrated editing tools used in a programming environment.

GameMaker: Studio is an application used by newcomers to game design and by experienced developers alike, for both personal and commercial purposes:

- This contains a very clean interface including a fully functional drag and drop programming interface making it very easy to get started creating games. Experienced GameMaker developers typically choose to create games using the text-based coding functionality of the built-in GML.

- This also contains many high-level functions and components for a variety of things that developers might need done in their game and for a variety of platforms. Examples include networking, Steamworks™ SDK support, in-app purchases, and more for platforms such as Microsoft Windows™, Apple Mac OS X™, Linux™ in terms of desktop and laptops, and Google Android™, and Apple iOS for mobile. Many more platforms are available for use with GameMaker: Studio.

- GameMaker: Studio has been used to create many commercial games, a varying selection of which you can view at http://yoyogames.com/showcase.

Choosing your version

GameMaker: Studio is available for download exclusively for Microsoft Windows at `http://yoyogames.com/studio`. There are a few different versions available, each adding more functionality as the price point increases. All of the versions allow you to create games using the game engine. For the most part, the increased functionality relates to publishing your game to different platforms as well as providing some additional features.

The Standard Edition is fully functioning and is perfectly adequate for developing games in GameMaker: Studio. The Professional Edition includes many more features than the Standard, such as team features, early access builds, the ability to purchase additional export modules, and allows the developer to publish games to platforms beyond Windows and **GameMaker: Player**. The Master Collection contains everything available, which is the Professional Edition bundled with all the export modules. The additional export modules cannot be purchased with only the Standard Edition of GameMaker: Studio.

Whatever version you choose, keep in mind its limitations and what you might need, but do not pay for more than you need. You might purchase the Master Collection and end up only using the additional HTML5 module, making the additional features unnecessary. However, keep in mind that you can commercially publish your games with any version of the IDE, but the Standard Edition will force a splash screen and application name that both say "Made with GameMaker: Studio".

You can always upgrade later, so the Standard version is a perfectly appropriate place to start. Once you've chosen your version, get a license key for it and download the GameMaker: Studio installer and run it.

> The following is a note about GameMaker: Studio licenses. The IDE will revalidate its license key with the YoYo Games servers once a month. However, if it cannot connect to them, you must manually relicense it with a special license file. Read more about this at `http://help.yoyogames.com/entries/27068613-Offline-Licence-Verification-for-GameMaker`.

The GameMaker: Studio interface

Now that you've completely installed GameMaker: Studio, let's begin learning some of the basics of GameMaker: Studio. Create a new game project by selecting the **New** tab at the top (after launching it), and choosing your project directory, as well as a name for this, we recommend testGame or something similar. Once your project is created, you should see a window, the GameMaker: Studio IDE, that looks quite similar to the one shown in the following screenshot:

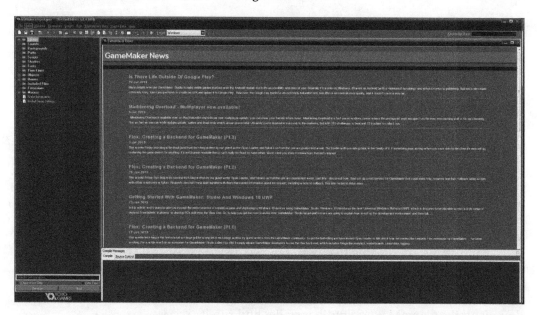

The left-hand side of the IDE consists of your resources, which is where all your sounds, sprites, rooms, scripts, and other resources can be found. Clicking on it simply selects them, and double-clicking will uncollapse folders and open up the properties of resources. Right-clicking on any of those folders will open a menu allowing you to create a new instance of the resource type. For example, right-clicking on the **Sprites** folder would give you the option to create a new sprite that you can edit and use in your game. If you right-click on **Scripts**, you can create a new script. Right-clicking on any of those folders also allows the creation of a new group, which is a subfolder strictly for organizational purposes. If a resource or group is right-clicked on, many more options will be available, such as renaming, editing properties, and so on. At the bottom of the resource tree are the **Game Information** and **Global Game Settings** options. The former is like a small notepad that you as the developer can write small notes or reminders for yourself in, but it is not packaged with the game.

The latter, the **Global Game Settings** option, will allow the editing of many properties of the game. When working with the Professional Edition or additional modules it contains, many additional settings that can be edited for specific targets and SDKs.

Along the top are various buttons, some of which are for creating resources (an alternative to right-clicking the folders on the left of the IDE) and others for game compilation options:

The green arrow is for regular compilation and testing, while the red one plays the game in debug mode with a **debugger** attached so as to view variables and other properties of the game as it runs to help you locate problems in your game. We'll teach you more about the debugger in *Chapter 9*, *Wrapping Up*. The brush is for cleaning the target, which comes in handy when you want to see if a glitch was caused by compilation issues or a fault in your code. The hot keys for these three buttons are *F5*, *F6*, and *F7*, respectively.

Everything from the *green Pac-Man* to the *white rectangle* and *inclusive*, are the buttons for creating resources. The next button is a button to access the **Global Game Settings**, mentioned previously. You can always hover your mouse over any of the buttons to see what they do.

The drop-down list all the way at the end of the top bar allows you to choose your target (or the OS for which your game should be compiled), which will vary based on what modules you may or may not have purchased. All will show up in the list regardless of what you bought, but Microsoft Windows and GameMaker: Player are the only ones that will actually work if you use the Standard Edition of GameMaker: Studio.

Additional keyboard shortcuts that you will find handy are *Ctrl* + *S* for saving, *Ctrl* + *N* to create a new project, and *Ctrl* + *O* for opening an existing project.

GameMaker: Studio documentation

One of the most important buttons on that bar is the question mark surrounded by a circle. Clicking on it opens the complete GameMaker documentation in a new window. It is a comprehensive reference for everything about the IDE, its functionality, drag and drop coding, GML coding, and all other aspects of GameMaker: Studio. It is very useful, and you will likely reference it often. This documentation can also be accessed at `http://docs.yoyogames.com/`. Additionally, when working in your code editor, if you put your cursor on one of GameMaker's built-in functions or variables, and click your middle mouse button, the documentation page for it will open so you can learn more about how to use it.

An example project

Now that you've got everything set up and you know some of your way around the IDE, let's start with an example game to get started with using GameMaker and to make sure everything is working correctly. You'll first want to create a new sprite, either by right-clicking on the **Sprites** folder and selecting **Create Sprite** or clicking on the *Pac-Man* symbol located on the top bar. This will open a new window that allows you to edit all of the properties of your new sprite. We're going to make a simple sprite that looks like a square.

> **Downloading the example code**
>
> You can download the example code files from your account at `http://www.packtpub.com` for all the Packt Publishing books you have purchased. If you purchased this book elsewhere, you can visit `http://www.packtpub.com/support` and register to have the files e-mailed directly to you.

Naming convention – resource prefixes

Start with naming it, but don't just name it `testSprite` or something like that. There are some very important points to be made in naming conventions of resources. It is a good idea to choose names that are related to the resources you are naming. The most important consideration is that your naming should be consistent regardless of the naming convention you choose. If you start using camelCase, always use it. camelCase is where the first letter of each name is lowercase, but every next word in the name has a capital first letter, for example, `myLastName` or `playerHorizontalSpeed`. If you always use underscores for naming (and this might be easier since GameMaker's built-in variables and functions use underscores for naming, an example of this would be the variable `image_index`), then always use underscores.

Also, you must never have spaces in any of your names because in coding, this would cause GameMaker to think they are two separate names and your game will not function properly. It is also good practice to follow and incorporate the resource prefixes. The GameMaker compiler does not recognize prefixes; they are simply part of the name, but all of your resources must have different names, as resource types are not distinguished by the compiler. Using prefixes is an easy way to group your resources though (so using `spr_player` and `obj_player` is better than `player` and `player1`).

Using the prefixes is also very helpful for you and any other programmers, since using them allows you to easily distinguish resource types. The resource prefixes are what help to distinguish between a sprite named `test` and an object named `test`. Also, make sure that you use meaningful names so that you can easily find what you're looking for or figure out what a resource is just by name. Following is a chart of the resource types and suggested prefixes. Eventually, you will have many resources in your games and will need to easily distinguish one from another.

Resource type	Acceptable prefix(es)	Example(s)
Sprites	spr or s	spr_test or s_test
Sounds	snd	snd_test
Backgrounds	bg	bg_test
Scripts	scr	scr_test
Fonts	fnt	fnt_test
Objects	obj or o	obj_test or o_test
Rooms	rm or lvl	rm_test or lvl_test

We recommend you use these prefixes when naming your resources, as they are universal and will help you to stay consistent in your naming. This is not a complete list of resources and prefixes but this table should give you a good sense of the naming convention.

Drawing the sprite

It's time to get started with sprites! Create your first sprite by right-clicking the **Sprites** folder and choosing **Create Sprite** or clicking on the *Pac-Man* icon in the toolbar. As discussed, we suggest naming your sprite spr_square or something similar, so enter that in the **Name** field. Next, you can select either the **Load Sprite** or **Edit Sprite** options. The first allows you to select an image that you already have saved on your computer, so select that if you already have an image of a square premade or prefer to use external programs for editing your sprites. GameMaker supports a wide array of image types including .bmp, .gif, .jpg, .png, and .swf. We're going to go through the built-in sprite editor, but in time, you will probably be using both approaches of sprite editing.

To start making your own images, you'll first have to click on **Edit Sprite**. Right now, the only thing you need to know how to do is to make a new **subimage** (more on these later) inside of your sprite. Click on the white dog-eared paper next to the green checkmark (which is the equivalent of *OK* in all windows and options in GameMaker: Studio). It will ask you what you want the dimensions of the image to be, which carry across all subimages in the sprite. Leave the 32 by 32 default alone for now—we're just making a simple square:

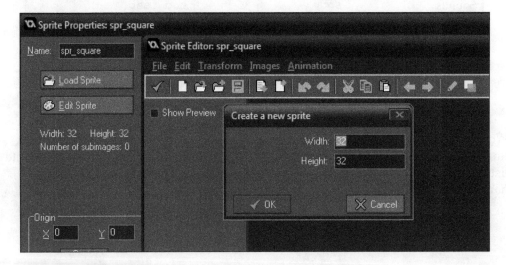

Now double-click on the new subimage that was created, which should be labeled as image 0, as GameMaker: Studio uses **zero-based indexing** (where the first entry of something, in this case subimages in a sprite, is entry 0), and the sprite editor will open, which should look like this:

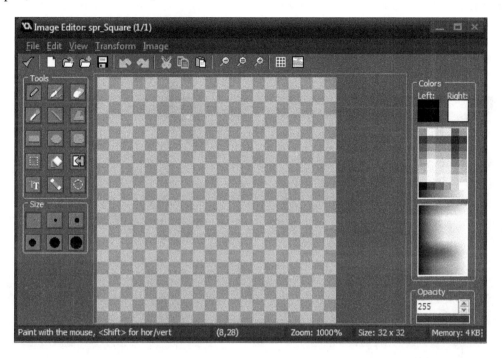

The left-hand side of the editor consists of your tools and dot sizes, while the right-hand side is your color picker. Two colors can be held at a time, one corresponding to each mouse button (left and right). As far as the tools, the most important ones would be the pencil for basic drawing, the eraser for erasing, the selection tool to select an area for manipulation, and the fill option to fill in an area with a single color. Hovering over any of these tools tells you their function and hotkey. We're only going to use one of these tools right now. Start making your square by selecting any color from the color picker. Next, use the fill option to fill in the entire grid with your selected color and then click on the green checkmark three times (in the three separate windows of course) to completely close out of the sprite and return to the main IDE.

Creating an object

Now that our sprite is finished up, we're going to create a basic object to put in our game. It is worth pointing out an important distinction here. Sprites are simply graphics to be used in your game while objects are programmed with events and actions in order to function in the game. Without an object, the game is just going to be an unchanging screen. Objects are what control and do everything in the game. Start with creating your object, named `obj_square` with your method of choice. The following window should appear:

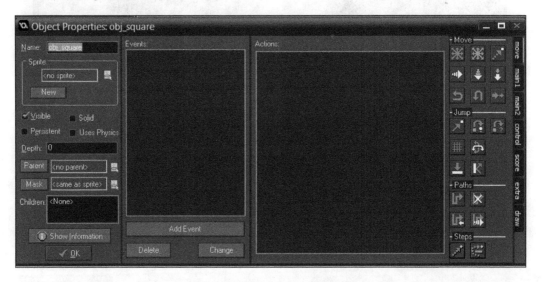

To assign a sprite to your object (which is not always necessary, in fact many objects in your games will not use sprites) select the blue button in the box labeled **Sprite** and pick the sprite we previously created, `spr_square`. Don't worry about anything else you see on the left sidebar, we will get into this in more detail later. For now, focus your attention on the first large box, labeled **Events**. Events are simply things that happen in your game, such as player input or when an instance of an object is created, and they are handled similarly to `if` statements, and run the associated *Action(s)*. Actions are the same as statements (what should happen based on the event). So one event might be a keypress of the space key, and when that occurs, the player should jump. In pseudo-code for that event, you might say, if the space key is pressed, then alter the player's *y* coordinate so that they rise. Then, once they've reached a certain point, change the *y* coordinate so that the player falls. Right now, we shall be putting an event into our game. Select the **Add Event** button at the bottom, select the **Draw** button, followed by the **Draw** menu option. This is a kind of event that is run over and over for each instance until the instance is destroyed (removed from the game), and is used for rendering. You can display whatever you want: shapes, text, sprites, and much more.

Another event, the **Step** event, is similar to this (it runs over and over) but it does not control rendering. You shouldn't use the **Draw** event as a replacement **Step** event though we use both together (or just one of them if you only need one of them).

Now focus on the right sidebar. This is where all of your available **Actions** are, and whatever you drag into the **Actions** pane will be run when the associated event occurs. Select the **draw** tab at the bottom of the list of tabs on the right and then drag the **Draw Self** box (the first *action*) into the **Actions** window. This will draw in the room the sprite of the instance of the object that is calling the function. You do not always need to use the function, but we do need it now because we have manually included a **Draw** event. If we don't include it, then the square won't be displayed; only whatever we tell it to display in the next step will be displayed. If you manually include a **Draw** event in your object, it will not draw its sprite and will only draw what you tell it to draw inside this event. So if we don't tell the object to draw itself in this event, you will see no squares drawn. Now, drag the **Draw Text** box, the fourth option or the first in the second row, into the **Actions** box:

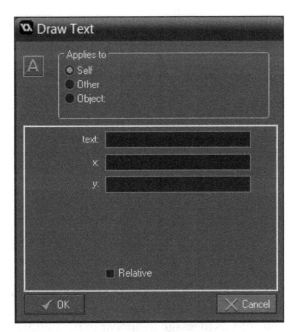

This should open up a box that looks like the one in the preceding screenshot where you can edit the arguments that you pass to the **Draw Text** function, which include, in this case, the text itself and the x/y coordinates where you want to draw the text. Edit the **text** field so that it holds, Hello, World! (no quotes) but do not enter anything into the **x** and **y** fields yet—there is something unexpected about these.

Coordinate planes in GameMaker

Typically, on a coordinate plane, your *x* value would increase as you move right and your *y* value would increase as you move up. This stays true for *x*, but not for *y*. For *y*, the value will increase as you move down, meaning that the fourth quadrant, which usually holds negative *y* values, will hold positive *y* values, and the first quadrant, usually holding positive *y* values, will hold negative *y* values. This is a very important note to remember when thinking about where things will be placed in your game. Although, do know that the room only exists in your fourth quadrant, and so what is shown on your screen is also only the fourth quadrant. However, everything can be placed anywhere, so you can actually place objects and whatever you draw at negative coordinates, but of course, either none or only a portion of whatever you have placed will be shown in the game window. A third (or *z*) axis does exist; it is called **depth** and refers to the placement of objects in your game in terms of being above and below each other. You will learn about this in depth in the next chapter. Here is a simple coordinate plane to explain this:

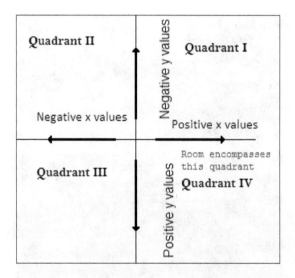

Now that you know this, we can resume passing arguments to the **Draw Text** function. For this example, we are going to have a room with dimensions of 1024 by 768 pixels, and we want this message to appear in the middle of the room, so we're going to pass an **x** value of 512 and a **y** value of 384 to the function. Do not select the **Relative** checkbox, as what this would do is have the message appear at (512, 348) relative to the origin of the square object, which, unless we put the object exactly in the top left corner of the room (which we won't), will have the message display somewhere not in the middle. Select the **OK** button twice to get back to the main IDE.

Creating a room

We're now going to create one more final resource, and that is a room. Without a room, the game will not compile, so you must always have at least one room, even if it is completely empty. A room is where your game takes place and where your objects are placed. While your objects control the mechanics of your game, they have to be placed in a room for them to actually be used. Create a room with your method of choice and name it rm_main or something similar. Many games contain sandbox or testing rooms that the player wouldn't have access to, and are just for testing various parts of your game. Even though we only have one object in our game and aren't really testing anything, you can think of this room as a testing room:

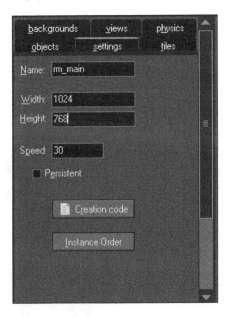

The default dimensions, which we will be using, are already set, as is the **room speed**, or how many times per second each object in the room runs its code. The room speed of 30 is perfectly fine for us right now. Select the **objects** tab on the left sidebar, and the only object we have, obj_square, will be already assigned to your left mouse button. Click anywhere in the room to place this object, and place more than one. For this example, 10 would be a good number. Click on the green checkmark when you are done, and you will have finished creating your first game in GameMaker: Studio.

Testing your game

Only one step is left, and that is compiling and running your game. Press *F5* on your keyboard or click on the green arrow on the top bar. This will begin the compilation process and then run your game. If everything worked correctly, then you should see a game window that looks similar to this, but with the squares wherever you placed them and in whatever color you chose for the sprite:

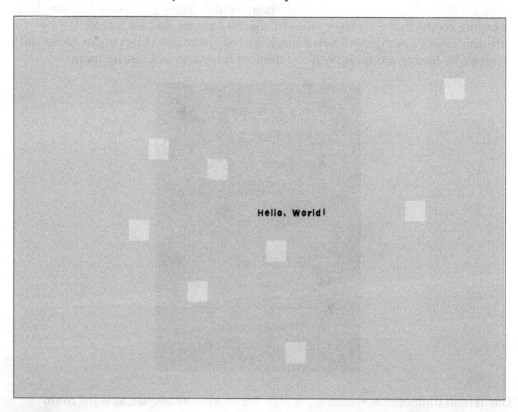

If your game window doesn't look like this, then check whether you followed all the instructions correctly (such as choosing the right event and the right parameters for your **Draw Text** action). You might want to check it with the sample code included with this book to ensure that everything is correct. If that doesn't work, perform a clean build with *F7* to make sure your next compilation will start completely fresh so that any compiler-induced errors will not occur. If both of those failed to help you, look at the compiler window at the bottom to see if it tells you anything about errors:

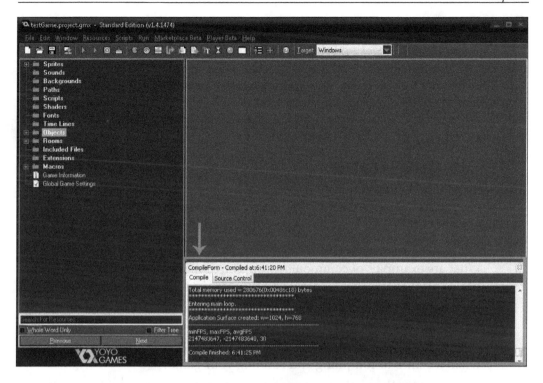

If none of these options work, then you might need to perform a fresh install of GameMaker: Studio. YoYo Games has provided an excellent guide for this, which is located at `http://help.yoyogames.com/entries/37903916-How-to-perform-a-fresh-install`.

What's happening here in the game is that one instance of the message **Hello, World!** and one instance of `obj_square` are being created for each instance of the object that you placed in the room. The top-left corner of the message is where the coordinates we put in earlier are applied, which is why the message isn't *precisely* in the center of the room. The reason that you only see one instance of that message rather than many is because we told all the objects to display a message at that *exact* location. In turn, all of these instances of the message are actually overlapping directly on top of one another.

Summary

Now that you have finished the chapter, you have a good understanding of the GameMaker: Studio interface. You have learned what many of the buttons on the main interface do; how to create and name resources including sprites, objects, and rooms; how to add events and actions to your objects and assign them sprites; how rooms and their coordinates work; and how to compile your games.

Review questions

It's always good to be asked questions so that you can be sure you comprehend everything you have read; so, here are some review questions to go over. If you can't figure one out, that's a sign that you could benefit from more reviewing of the chapter:

- What are examples of common naming conventions used for the various resources available in GameMaker: Studio?

- How do you open the documentation for GameMaker: Studio and what is it useful for?

- What is the difference between the green play button and the red play button when it comes to compiling and running your game?

- How do coordinate planes in rooms here vary from the Cartesian coordinate system (regular mathematics)?

- What are events and actions and how are they related?

Quick drills

It's also good for comprehension to apply the skills you learned in different ways, so here are some little challenges that you can try out to make sure you understand how to perform the tasks you learned:

1. Edit the sprite in your spr_square and play around with some of the other tools in the editor to modify your original image (your final outcome doesn't even have to be a square); just rename the sprite to reflect this, as with your object.

2. Play around with some of the other actions on your obj_square to make it do more rather than be displayed and print text. Try something and immediately test it. It will become good practice to test your games often in order to discover errors where they originate. If you add ten features and discover a bug, you don't know where it came from—but if you add one and get a bug, you know where your problem is.

3. Create a new project named testGame2 or something like that. It will be a clone of the original example, but you're not going to reread the instructions in the chapter or read them from your example game. You're instead going to see if you can recall how to do everything from memory. If you can't recall something, review the chapter to make sure you are comfortable with the content.

Remember that all of these drills and questions are for your comprehension and you're good, so do them — it only helps. With that, this chapter concludes and hopefully, you learned a lot about using GameMaker: Studio. The next chapter will cover the creation of a more complex game with which the player interacts. It will be an escape the dungeon game from which you will learn all sorts of components of programming games in GameMaker: Studio, much more so than you already know about.

An extra note that you might find helpful — GameMaker saves backups of your game by default in your Documents\GameMaker\Backups\<project name> folder. You might find that it saves them far too often and does not save enough, so under the **File** option in the IDE's top bar, select **Preferences**, and the left pane will allow you to specify some backup-related options (frequency, location, and amount). Backups are useful if you accidentally break your game and need to go back to a point where everything worked. It might be helpful to make a copy of a working project alongside using the built-in backup system.

2
Your First Game – Escape the Dungeon

In this chapter, you will start to really learn about creating games in the GameMaker: Studio IDE. The last game you made was rather simple and did not have much to it. However, in this chapter, you will be creating a basic dungeon escape game. You will be guided through a step-by-step process and then have an opportunity to expand upon your game and make it your own. This type of game will teach you many skills that will apply to many other games and serves as a solid foundation with regard to the basic use of GameMaker. You'll learn about player input, collision, health, movement, resources, variables, and a variety of other topics. This *Escape the Dungeon* example will provide a good experience in the use of the GameMaker IDE and its drag and drop coding interface. It also serves to segue into the GML, which you will begin to utilize in the next chapter.

Creating your Escape the Dungeon game

Your *Escape the Dungeon* game is going to be a simple 2D maze-like game where the player dodges enemies and escapes a labyrinth of sorts to proceed through the levels. Your player will be able to shoot at these enemies and the enemies in turn will shoot randomly. In addition, the player will need to collect keys to unlock doors to the next level. This will introduce the use of variables in the game. The game is fairly simple, but teaches many skills in terms of using GameMaker: Studio.

First, create a new game project called `EscapeTheDungeon` by selecting the **New** tab at the very start screen of GameMaker: Studio. Choose your directory and project name. The GameMaker IDE should then open in a new workspace.

The playable character

The playable character is something that has a few components that make it up. It is an object that the user of the game will control via keyboard input that can allow it to move in four directions and shoot. The player consists of a sprite and an object that has many events and actions. It starts with the creation of the main sprite and its individual subimages. Next is creating an object that is programmed based on events and actions in GameMaker: Studio. The object can receive input from the player and monitor what is going on in the game so that it can react appropriately to the different possible situations. In this game, there are a number of things that the player needs to do, including moving and shooting.

The sprite

Follow these steps for creating a sprite:

1. Start creating your game by making a new sprite named spr_PC where **PC** stands for **Playable Character**.

2. Select the **Edit Sprite** option, and then select the same button we used before to create a new subimage – the white dog-eared paper on the top bar. Give it the dimensions of 32 by 64, after which a new image 0 will be created. Double-click on it to open it up in the sprite editor and draw a semi-top view of your character. A semi-top view would mean that you combine a top-down view with a frontal view. It doesn't have to look perfect.

3. After you have finished drawing it, you will want to resize the canvas so that it completely fits the player sprite. But first, select the actual content of the player sprite and move it to the top-left corner so that the top and left edges of the sprite touch the top and left edges of the canvas. Next, you can resize the canvas. To do this, you click on **Transform** at the top, followed by **Resize Canvas**. You can also use the keyboard shortcut *Ctrl + Alt + C*. A window that looks like the following screenshot will appear:

4. You probably won't keep the **aspect ratio** (which is the original ratio of width to the height of the sprite), so uncheck that box. The box with all the arrows that you see at the bottom right defines which region/direction of the sprite will be kept when resizing. Because we put the sprite into the top-left corner, the one that you would choose is the top-left arrow. In that way, resizing the canvas will eliminate from the bottom-right corner and keep the top left safe, provided that you don't eliminate too much. Note that you will be changing which arrow you select after a few resizes, as you might have finished resizing one side, but not the other.

5. Start with decreasing the pixel amounts (at the top on the right side) in small amounts. The left side is the percent of the canvas to get rid of, but that can be hard to guess, so pixels are usually good, particularly for such small sprites. Don't go overboard making the canvas smaller—if you do it too much, some parts of your image will be deleted. You can always undo a resize, but it's better to not have to. Change the arrow that you have selected as you go along and keep resizing until the canvas perfectly matches the sprite. Your canvas most likely won't be proportional to its original size; the lengths probably won't be powers of two nor will they be even, but that is still fine—in fact it's better to perfectly resize your canvas to get rid of as much whitespace as possible. If you don't, problems with collision events (more on this later) might occur when playing your game.

Once you have finished creating that subimage, you're going to create three more. But this requires a different button. The first button that you used was responsible for creating the first subimage of the sprite, labeled `image 0`. But using that button again will erase the existing `image 0` and create a new one. So instead, to add `image 1`, `image 2`, `image 3`, ..., and image *n* you will use the button that is five buttons after the original one you used. It should appear as a white paper with a plus logo at the top right corner. The one directly next to it on the left, with the down arrow at the bottom right of it, adds a new subimage directly before the one that you have currently selected (the one selected will be highlighted in blue), and will thus rename the affected subimages so that the names are always in numbered order.

There's also the option to select a subimage and then press *Ctrl + C* to copy it, then *Ctrl + V* to paste it, which you may choose to do instead of using the aforementioned buttons in the following step so that you have a vantage point.

6. Create three new subimages with the new button with the plus logo. They should all be images of the player, but from different views. Make `image 1` a view of the back, `image 2` a view of the right, and `image 3` a view of the left.

7. For your left and right orientations, you can simply copy the entire canvas of one of them, paste it into the other, then select **Transform** followed by **Mirror/Flip** (which can also be accessed by pressing *Ctrl + Alt + M*). Then make sure **Mirror Horizontally** is checked and hit the checkmark button.

8. Don't resize your canvas unless you need to make it slightly bigger – the canvas size remains the exact same for each subimage, so you can end up with whitespace by increasing the size. Your final outcome should have subimages with views that look like the following:

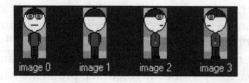

With this, you have completed your sprite for the playable character. Next is creating the object.

The object

Now that your sprite for the playable character has been completed, you should create its object. Start off with creating and naming the object something like `obj_PC` and then assign a sprite to it. Next, add the event labeled as **Keyboard**, then select **<Left>**, at the top of the list. You probably noticed the other key-related events when looking at the list of events, shown in the following screenshot:

The following is a table to show the differences between these three key-related events:

Keyboard	Key Press	Key Release
This checks over and over if a key is pressed and repeats its associated action as long as the key is pressed	This checks once to see if a key is pressed and runs its associated action once for each press	This checks to see if a key has been released and runs its associated action based on if the particular key has been released
While pressing, the action is run many times	One press and the action runs once	One release and the action runs once

Okay, so now that you understand the difference between these key-related events, you can start working on your **Keyboard** event for the left arrow key.

1. The first tab on the right, labeled **move**, contains a section also named **Move** that has an action called **Move Fixed**. It is the first option and its image looks like eight green arrows diverging from the center. Drag that into the **Actions** box for the keyboard event.

2. The parameter window will open. Because this is a **Keyboard** event for the left arrow key, we will select the left arrow in the grid. This will make the object move towards the left. Next, change **speed** to 3. This defines how fast an object is moving.

3. Once you've passed your **Move Fixed** action and its required parameters, select the **main1** tab at the side, and under the **Sprite** section, drag the first option – **Change Sprite** – into the **Actions** box so that it runs before the **Move Fixed** event.

4. Your parameters consist of the main sprite from which to pull a subimage, the subimage itself to pick, and the speed. First select the sprite for the player you created earlier. Next, because the subimage for the left side of our character is labeled `image` 3, put 3 into the subimage box. The speed refers to how fast the subimages of the sprite will be cycled through, but because we only want the left image to be displayed while moving left, set that to 0 as shown in the following screenshot:

5. Now, add a **Key Release** event, and again select **<Left>**. This is for when the player stops pressing the left key, and thus, we want them to stop moving. Drag a **Move Free** action, the gray option right next to **Move Fixed**, into the **Actions** box.

The **direction** parameter refers to which direction the object should be facing, so that means up, down, left, or right. But you don't pass it to any of those words, you pass it a number or a special variable called `direction`. The numbers corresponding with right, up, left, and down are 0, 90, 180, or 270 respectively. The following diagram is to show the direction values, which you will directly use sometimes:

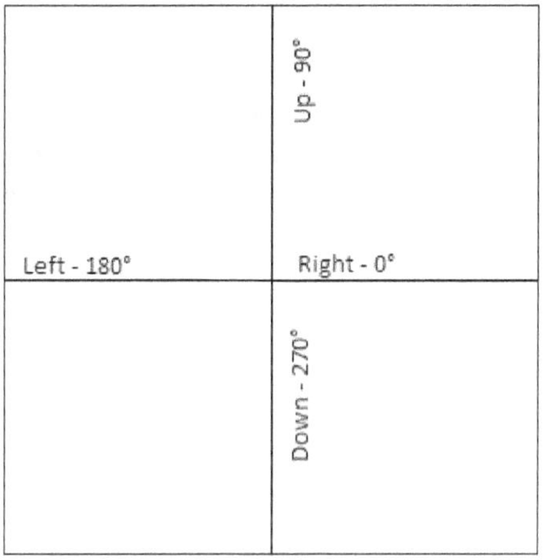

	Up - 90°
Left - 180°	Right - 0°
	Down - 270°

But you shouldn't be using those numbers here either. Instead, use the built-in `direction` variable. It is a special variable that every object has and refers to the direction the object is facing. In this way, you don't necessarily have to know their direction—you can just pass this variable.

So, type `direction` (no quotes) into the **direction** box, and put 0 into the **speed** box, so that the player will stop moving after you release the *Left* key. Now, repeat this process for each of the other keys, substituting in the correct directions and subimages, where needed, so that, you can control your player in all four directions. Exit from the player object and create a new room. Insert one instance of the player object anywhere in the room, and then run your game.

What did you notice? Probably that on startup, the player cycles through all the subimages really fast. But that's not what you want, right? You want them to be set on one subimage at startup. And this is where the **Create** event comes in handy.

Go back to your `obj_PC` and add a **Create** event. This is run every time the instance of the object is created. It's good for setting up things such as variables that you'll need later or setting things up so they don't bug out or anything. Drag in another **Change Sprite** action into the **Actions** box, and pick whatever subimage you want — we recommend `image 0`, the down facing subimage. Again, make sure that **speed** is 0 there, so that it doesn't still cycle through the subimages. Run your game again, and your object should stay on the first subimage until you press a key other than *Down*. This is because we basically initialized the sprite so that it would be set to a specific one. We decided what the starting sprite would be. So great, you've got the movement and changing sprite based on direction functionality. It is a rather basic system, as you can probably notice, given that most people move their legs when walking along, but this is a good enough system to use to at least teach the basics.

Walls

Okay, so you've got your player moving, but so far the game is pretty boring. There's nothing to do except move around a blank screen. We could add enemies, but there's a fundamental problem in the game that needs fixing now. There are no walls, and thus the player can just walk off screen. They won't fall off some kind of an edge or anything, they'll be able to walk right back in; but most games don't have that ability. So, we need to add some walls.

Start with making your wall sprite: `spr_wall`. It should be 32 by 32 pixels and at least somewhat resemble a wall. This sprite needs only one subimage: the wall, and once you've finished making it, you can start on the object. The object is also very simple. Create the object, name it, and assign it a sprite. But there's one more thing you have to do — set it as solid. Setting it as solid will allow the player to collide with it, that is, a collision event inside of the player will recognize only solid objects; otherwise, they will just pass right through, which we don't want. Voilà, you've finished making the object.

That doesn't mean you're done with walls yet though. You need to add another event to the player object that occurs when they hit (collide with) a wall. Open up the player object and add a new **Collision** event, selecting your wall object when it prompts you. This event will be triggered whenever the player hits an instance of the wall. Earlier, whenever the player stopped pressing an arrow key, we wanted the player object to stop. Like before, drag in the **Move Free** action, and set the variable as `direction` and **speed** as 0. Your player will now stop short whenever it hits a wall. Open up your room and put walls all around the room. Next, create a sort of maze through which the player must traverse, and move your player to the starting point (if it is not already there). Test your game.

My player object is sometimes getting stuck even though it shouldn't! How do I fix this?

Depending on the size of your player sprite, your player might be colliding with the wall because the wall's width is 32 pixels and one grid space is 32 pixels, so spaces between two blocks could be 32 pixels. When the player tries to get through these spaces, it could be brushing up against the walls, and thus colliding, getting them stuck.

The way to fix this is to first make sure that you resized the canvas or cropped the image to fit the player sprite exactly. Test your game, and if the problem no longer arises, then you've fixed your problem. Otherwise, you can open up the sprite, select **Transform**, and then **Stretch** (which can also shrink the sprite, as we will be doing here). You can also use the keyboard shortcut *Ctrl + Alt + E*. Select whatever quality you want of the outcome in relation to the original, although the default **Normal** option is fine, and then decrement the dimensions in small amounts until you think it's small enough. Just make sure it's smaller than the smallest space it needs to get through. Test the game out, and see if the problem persists. If it still does, continue to shrink the canvas with **Stretch** until the problem is fixed.

My player object is stopping even though it's not touching the wall! How do I fix this?

Your player might be supposedly colliding with the wall even though you see a few pixels in front of it. This is because **basic collision checking** in GameMaker goes by the dimensions of the whole dimensions of the sprite itself. It uses the largest dimensions, and will always be a rectangle. The head or another region of your player is most likely protruding outwards compared to other parts, and thus there are blank spots that still count for collisions. The way to fix this is to use **precise collision checking**, where the **collision mask** (the shape used for a particular sprite by GameMaker to determine if there is a collision) used by the sprite, follows the shape of the subimages exactly. This will solve your problem.

To utilize precise collision checking, go back to your player sprite's window. Click on the checkbox next to **Precise collision checking** under the box labeled **Collision Checking**. The only disadvantage of this here, at least in this case, is that the player object might get stuck on a wall (if their body is completely touching the wall) and you will have to move left or right to move at all. There are some cases in which it is bad to use, such as the aforementioned and as it is slower than regular collision checking, but it is fine here. When you move on though, you are likely to stop using precise collision checking, given its downsides, and alternative collision checking methods.

Enemies

Okay, so your player moves, changes sprite based on direction, and we've put in a maze. But the game is still boring. We need to add some enemies and a health property to the player so that they can be damaged by these enemies. Create your sprite in a similar manner to what you did with the player, in that, there are four subimages for each of the enemy's directions, and do it in the same order as you did for the player. This enemy is going to either walk up and down or left and right.

Once you have completed your enemy's sprite, create two objects named obj_enemyVert and obj_enemyHor, for their walking patterns. Make sure to set both of them as **solid**, by selecting the checkbox, as when the player hits the enemy, we want a collision event to be triggered (thus requiring **solid**). As we had previously with the player, make sure you have a **Create** event for each enemy. Add the **Change Sprite** action to it so that the object does not cycle through its entire sprite's subimages before moving. Your enemy will start moving immediately, so this is not entirely necessary, but it is a good habit to indicate the starting direction and subimage for objects that will move in your game. This is important in case the enemy is somehow noticeably slow as it initializes and starts to walk, where we will handle more of the sprite changing code.

Making your enemies move

In your horizontally (left and right) moving enemy, under the **Create** event, add a **Move Fixed** action. Select both the left and right arrows. What this does is, it makes the game choose between either the left or right directions. So your object could start moving left, or it could start moving right. Set **speed** to 2, slightly slower than our player.

Next, add a **Collision** event, and choose **obj_Wall**. When the enemy hits a wall, we want it to reverse its direction. To do this, we select the **Reverse Horizontal** action; it's under the **Move** section under the **move** tab on the left and is the first option in the third row, with a green arrow pointing towards the left. There are no parameters or anything to provide this action with, so you can just add it and be done.

Now, we want to change the sprite of the enemy, but we have to be able to tell what direction they are facing. Luckily, there is the built-in direction variable. To test its value, we will use a **Test Variable** action, located under **control**, then **Variables**. It is the middle option—an octagonal square. The variable we want to test is direction, and the value we want to test it for is 0. Remember that 0 represents the right direction. So if direction is equal to 0 (that is, the enemy is moving to the right), then the following action should be run.

In order to have the next action run based on whether `direction` equals 0, we will use **Start** and **End** blocks. These are like curly braces, {}, in text-based coding. In the **control** tab, under **Other**, there are two triangles. The one whose point is facing upwards is a **Start** block, the equivalent of the {, and the one whose point is facing downwards is an **End** block, the equivalent of the }. Drag both of these underneath the **Test Variable** action.

Inside the triangle blocks, place a **Change Sprite** action and change the object's subimage so that it is one of the enemies moving to the right. Now, we want a similar thing to occur if the object is moving to the left, which happens when the object is not moving right, and thus whenever the object is not moving right, it is moving left. That seems obvious, but it's important. This means, we can just use an **Else** block and not have to test any more conditions. Drag in an **Else** block, located next to the **Start** block. Then, drag two **Start** and **End** blocks beneath it.

Put in a **Change Sprite** action (inside those blocks) so that the object's subimage will change to that of the enemy moving left. Now, the object's image will be altered based on its direction. However, this so far only happens when the object hits a wall. When they first are moving, they won't necessarily have the right subimage displayed. To fix this, copy all of the actions from the testing of the direction variable (not the reversing of it) down to the last **End** block we just made under the **Collision** event with the wall, and then, paste it underneath the **Move Fixed** action in the **Create** event. You can select the **Test Variable** action, then press *Shift* and click on the last **End** block to highlight all of it, and then use *Ctrl + C* to copy it and *Ctrl + V* to paste it. Now the subimage will always reflect the direction.

There's only one more thing we have to fix. As of now, the two enemies can collide and pass through each other. To fix this, add two **Collision** events, one for each version of the enemy. Copy all the actions from the **Collision** with the wall event and paste it into these two new **Collision** events. Now the enemies will "reflect" off each other.

In the end, all of your **Collision** events for the horizontally moving enemy should look like the following. In your **Create** event, what is here from lines 2 through 9 should appear directly following the **Move Fixed** action.

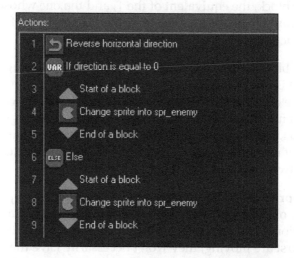

Repeat this entire process for the other version of the enemy—the one that moves up and down. Change actions, parameters, and such as needed to reflect the different directions. The **Reverse Vertical** action is on the right of the **Reverse Horizontal** action; remember that 0 represents right, 90 is up, 180 is left, and 270 is down. Test your game and make sure everything is working perfectly. If it's not, then go back and make sure you used the right parameters and actions and you put them everywhere that they should be.

Damaging the player

Now that the movement is working in your player and enemies, you can program in a health and damage system. The way that this will work is that whenever the player hits an instance of the enemy, their health will be decremented. If their health runs out, then they will lose a life and must restart.

To implement this system, first go to the **Create** event for your player. Now go to the **score** tab, and under the **Health** section, drag out the first option: **Set Health**. Give it a value of 100. Since health is a built-in global variable, there is only one of it and any uses of it will refer to that variable. Thus, you cannot give both your player and enemy a variable for health named health; for that, you might want to give the enemy one of your own variables, such as hp.

Next, create two **Collision** events inside the player, one for each type of enemy.
Drag out another set **Health** action for each, and give it a value of -25. Then, select
the **Relative** checkbox. Whenever the player collides with either enemy, their health
will be set *relative* to -25, meaning it will be decremented by 25.

Now, select the **move** tab and drag out a *Jump to Start* action (the second one under
the **Jump** section) for each **Collision** event. There are no parameters for this one, so
you can drag it out and be done. At this point, whenever the player hits an enemy,
their health will be decremented and they will jump to their starting position in the
room. The reason we have them move is because if neither the enemy nor the player
moves or dies, then the player's health will continue to decrement as long as they
are colliding with the enemy, and they will lose all their health in less than a second,
which would of course not be good.

Okay, so we have the basic health system working. But the player needs to *die*
and the health needs to be displayed. To do this, create a new object called obj_
healthControl. This is a **controller object**, a kind of object that doesn't necessarily
appear visually in your game, but controls variables, timing, and other important
elements of your game that it could not work without. Controller objects are nothing
more than a regular object, they're not recognized by the GameMaker: Studio
compiler or anything like that, but using them is a common approach developers use
to control aspects of the game that do not require a visible sprite in the game. When
objects without sprites (which are most often controller objects) are placed in the
room editor, they will appear (to the developer) as a blue circle with a question mark
inside to indicate their presence in the game.

Now you will add a new event. Select the **Other** option, then **No more health**. This
will be triggered when the health is less than or equal to 0. It is not always the best
approach to use, as you might want the player to die when their health is less than
1 (maybe the health is 0.75), but for our purposes here it is fine, given the value of
the total health and the values that can be decremented from it. The other approach
would be to use a **Test Variable** action and test to see if the variable (in this case
health) is less than 1.

In this example, when the player's health is eliminated, we want the game to end or restart, based on what the player chooses. To do this, we will ask them a question. Select the **control** tab, and then under **Questions**, pick the action whose symbol is a question mark inside of a bubble; have it say, You have died. Restart?. Now drag out a **Start** and **End** block. Inside, place a **Restart Game** action, located in the **Game** section under the **main2** tab. So, if the player says yes to restarting, the game will restart. Now drag out an **Else** block and a **Start** and **End** block. If the player answered no, then they want the game to end. So drag out an **End the game** action, located directly next to the **Restart the game** action:

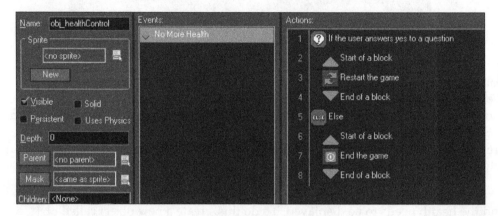

Great, now the game restarts or ends when the player dies. But the user needs to know what their health is and not have to think about or remember it. This is a simple implementation. Add one more event, a **Draw** event, like the one we used previously. Inside, drag a **Draw Health** action, the third option under **Health** under the **score** tab. **x1** refers to the *x* coordinate of the top-left corner, **y1** to the *y* coordinate of the top-left corner, **x2** to the *x* coordinate of the bottom-left corner, and **y2** to the *y* coordinate of the bottom-left corner. **back color** refers to the background color of the bar, and **bar color** is what color the actual bar itself will fade from and to as the health decreases. The length of the bar should be a multiple of 10, as the health variable is at most 100, and the health bar needs to look clean. It also needs to look full when the health is 100. For this game, the length of the health bar will be 50 pixels. To do this, set the value of **x1** to 10, and the value of **x2** to 60. The height of the bar should be 20 pixels, so set **y1** to 10 and **y2** to 30. Recall that in GameMaker's coordinate planes, *y* increases as you move down, not up. The background color of the bar should be black so that the player knows how much health they have in relation to the whole amount they could have, and the bar color that you choose can be anything you like. Do not select the **Relative** checkbox, as then you would need to very precisely place the healthControl object.

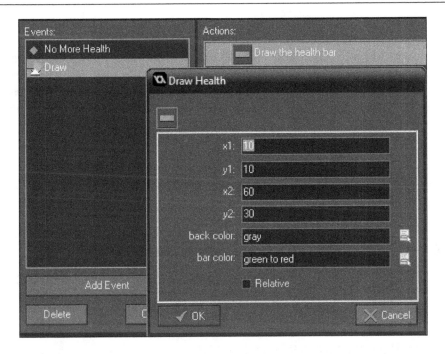

You might think that now adding the health control object to the room will display the health and the player will see their health and the bar will get shorter as they hit enemies more. This is, however, not necessarily true. The problem is that the health bar might be displayed below some wall or something because it is rendered before the wall, putting the wall on top. There is a simple fix, and you do not need to destroy any walls. Instead, you can set the depth of your health control object and, in turn, that of anything it draws, in this case, a health bar. Depth, as you should recall from the previous chapter is basically the rendering order of your objects. How large or small the number that you set it to does not matter, as depth is relative. In depth, the object with the largest depth number is rendered first, and the object with the smallest depth number is rendered last. It does not matter if those numbers are 1 and -1 or 1000 and -1000, they will be rendered in the same order. To set the depth of your healthControl object and thus make the health bar appear on top of everything else, change the **Depth** option beneath the four checkboxes on the left side of your object to -10. If you were to set another object's depth to -11, then the health bar would appear below that, but assuming you didn't, this health bar will be on top of everything. While you could just use -1, multiples of 10 are so much nicer to work with. Now the health bar will work perfectly.

Play your game and get hit four times by an enemy. Make sure that the question appears to restart, and click both buttons to make sure everything is working correctly. Also, observe your health bar. When you died, you might notice that the last quarter of the health bar does not disappear. This is because the **Draw** event is run after the **No more health** event, so the game will notice that the player has died and thus restart or end the game before it clears the health bar. This unfortunately cannot be fixed with drag and drop programming, but you will be able to solve it with the programming language of GameMaker, which you will soon learn about in the following chapter.

In the following chapter, some more features will be added to the health system that we have in place (such as pickups).

Making the player and enemies shoot

Now that you have the basics of your player, enemies, and health working, we can add one more feature that builds on all three of these – firing shots. The player and the enemy will fire in different ways from each other.

Making the player shoot

We'll start with working on the player's shooting mechanics. Start with making an 8 x 8 sprite for the bullet or whatever. It needs only one subimage, and you can just make a simple ball.

Now create an object for your bullet. Add a **Collision** event for each of the enemies. Whenever it collides with an enemy, it should destroy itself and the enemy it is colliding with. To do this, go to the **main1** tab, and drag out two of the **Destroy Instance** actions (that is two for each **Collision** event), which looks like a white recycle bin (a white bin with two curved green arrows forming a circle). The first one will destroy the bullet, so you can leave that alone. But the second one needs to destroy the enemy. The way to do this is to select the **Other** circle under the **Applies to** box at the top of the action's box. The three options there are **Self**, **Other**, and **Object**. Here is a table to explain the differences between the options:

Self	Other	Object
The instance of the object that you are working in	The instance of the object that you are interacting with	All instances of a particular object

Make sure that you did this for the **Collision** event with *each* enemy.

Great, so now whenever the bullet hits an enemy, it will kill both itself and the enemy. There's just one more **Collision** we have to add, and that is between the wall and the bullet. The bullet should not be able to go through the wall, so add a **Collision** event with the wall inside of the bullet, and when this happens, the bullet should destroy itself, just like with the enemy. You would not want to destroy the other in this case or you would destroy the wall. There might be times where you would want to be able to destroy select walls, such as if it is blocking a path that you want to get through, but not in our example here.

Now, the bullet for the player will work if it hits an enemy, but we still need to program it to be fired by your main character. We will do this inside of the player. Firstly, let's discuss how the shooting will work. The bullets should be fired when the player hits the spacebar, but we do not want the player to fire a continuous stream of bullets. To start this off, declare a new variable inside of the **Create** event for the player called `can_shoot`, and set it to 1. Use the **Set Variable** action, the first under the **Variables** section under the **control** tab. 1 refers to true in programming, and 0 to false. Whenever `can_shoot` is 0, the player cannot shoot, but they can if `can_shoot` equals 1:

Now add a new **Keyboard** event for the spacebar. When the player hits the spacebar, if `can_shoot` is equal to 1, the game should spawn a bullet near the player and temporarily prevent them from shooting for one second. First, drag out a **Test Variable** action and have it tested to see whether `can_shoot` is equal to 1. Also, drag out your **Start** and **End** blocks. To spawn the bullet, put a **Create Moving** action (the light bulb with a green arrow under **Objects** under the **main1** tab) inside your **Start** and **End** blocks. Have it create an instance of the player's bullet at the exact center of the player, and make sure that you select the **Relative** checkbox. Because nobody should be able to run faster than or at the same speed as a bullet, set **speed** to 5, which is greater than the speed of both the enemy and player. Bullets should travel in the same direction as the direction in which you are moving, so the direction variable should be used for the direction parameter. Note that direction is local to each instance of each object.

Now, we need to work out a system where the player must wait before shooting another bullet. First, set the variable `can_shoot` to 0 beneath the **Create Moving** action so that they cannot shoot until we assign it a value of 1 again. To do this, we'll use an alarm. These are timers that count steps, and they are local to each instance of each object. The number of steps per second is equal to the speed of your room. We are going to have that be 30 for this game, thus meaning that there will be 30 steps a second. Recall that room speed refers to how many times per second the objects in the room check their code, and thus, every object will check its code *room speed* steps every second. It is imperative to note that changing the room speed will change the number of steps per second, and thus know how long you have to set your alarms for. To create an alarm, drag the first option, the clock, under **Timing** under the **main2** tab. Set the number of steps to 30, as we want the player to have to wait one second before being able to fire again. Use the default `Alarm 0`. Make sure you did all of that inside of the **Start** and **End** blocks associated with your **Test Variable** action:

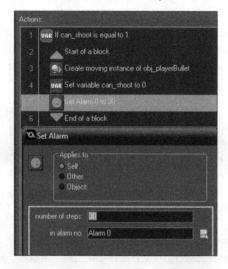

Next, add an **Alarm** event, and again use `Alarm 0`. When `Alarm 0` is triggered, the variable `can_shoot` should be set to 1 so that the player can shoot again.

And there you have it. Your player can now shoot and your enemies should disappear when you hit them. Test your game to make sure everything is functioning correctly.

Making the enemies shoot

Now that your player can shoot, we should make your enemies shoot. It's mostly the same. First create a sprite for the enemy bullet and make it a different color from that of your player to distinguish the two. Keep the same size though as our player bullet, 8 x 8 pixels.

Now create a new object for the enemy's bullet. Whenever it collides with a wall or the player, it should destroy itself. But it should also decrement the health variable by 15 (or whatever amount of health you choose to subtract. Just make sure that the value of health will always be an integer, as the way we are currently handling, dying is that when health is less than or equal to *0, not 1*, then, and only then, will the game restart prompt appear) when it collides with the player. It is very important that it destroys itself upon collision with the player, as otherwise, it would continuously damage the player and they would be dead in less than a second.

Now that your bullet object has been made, you need the enemy to be able to fire it. The way it will do this is randomly. There will be a chance that the enemy shoots a bullet, and a chance that it doesn't. To do this, create a new **Step** event in each of your enemy objects. When it asks for what kind of step, select **Step** again. Recall that there are 30 steps per second for this game. Therefore, ideally, all of your **Step** events will be run thirty times every second. However, this is only ideal. Depending on how much code is in your **Step** event and how many things the engine has to handle at once, your **Step** events might only be run 29 or 28 and so on times a second. This can make a difference, but in a case such as this, it doesn't matter quite so much. As long as the event is still run a good amount of times every second, you should be fine. If you ever run into complications with this, find ways to refine your code blocks when using drag and drop, and regular code in future chapters. You will become more efficient in your programming as you get more comfortable with GameMaker. Even cleaning up the smallest of things can make quite a difference.

Anyway, inside of your **Step** event, for both objects, add a **Test Chance** action, the middle option that looks like a green die under **Questions** in the **control** tab. Type 20 into the **sides** parameter. There will be a 1 in 20 (5 percent) chance that a bullet will be spawned each step, so with 30 steps per second, the enemy should shoot 3 times every 2 seconds (on average). Drag out your **Start** and **End** blocks, then a **Create Moving** action in between these. Spawn an instance of the enemy's bullet at the center of it. The speed should be 5, and the direction is the value of the direction variable. Make sure to check the **Relative** checkbox. Also, make sure that you did this for both enemy objects:

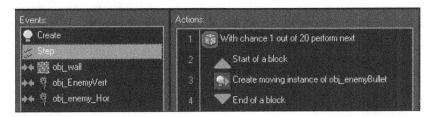

And with that, you have finished the shooting feature for both your player and enemies. Test out your game and make sure that the firing system is working for both, your player and enemy. Change the chance of shooting in the step event to see how it impacts the gameplay if you increase or decrease it. Do the same for the steps in the **Alarm** event for your player.

More resources

Alright, so all of the features of your game are working perfectly. You've got movement, collisions, a damage system, and bullets. But the game lacks some pizzazz. And that pizzazz comes in the form of more resources. Of all the resources on that resource tree that you can use, only three have been used. But we can use so many more. For now, we're just going to add a background and sounds.

Backgrounds

Every time you've played your game so far, the *background* of your game was just plain gray, which is quite boring. So instead, you can create your own backgrounds, or download them from somewhere (if you are downloading them, you need to be aware of copyright laws and ensure that you are permitted to use the image if you plan to publish your game, not this one but others). When you're downloading it, make sure that the image is proportional to 1024 x 768, otherwise it could appear to loop (which is sometimes good, if a background is intended to repeat) if you do not choose to stretch it. Of course, sometimes stretching/warping it can make it appear strange, whether the image is too small or too large. Just ensure that it's a good background that will look right to you. Of course, it's not of high importance in this game though, this is just an example to teach you how to use GameMaker's background capabilities.

Now, we will go through the process of adding a background. Create your new background and use the naming convention bg_<name>. If you downloaded it or made it with an external program, click on **Load Background** and navigate to the image file. Otherwise, use the built-in editor and make something. The dimensions should be 1024 by 768, as those are the dimensions of our room. It doesn't need to be perfect, as this is just a simple test game and if you are on a development team, there is probably a graphic artist to handle sprites and backgrounds in commercially published games.

Once you've finished creating the background, you can add it to your game. To do this, open up your room and select the **backgrounds** tab. First, select the checkbox that says **Visible when room starts**. Then select your background via the button underneath the **Foreground** image checkbox. Voilà, your background will have been added:

Sounds

Sounds can completely change a game. Some games are even critically acclaimed for their soundtracks. They also can serve as things to notify the player that something has happened (for example, they have hit a wall, or their score was incremented, and so on). We will overview the second use of sounds rather than create soundtracks, but the first is quite easy to stem from this.

We will create a few sounds for when an enemy dies, when the player gets hit, and when the player advances to the next room (which we will implement at the last stage of this chapter). Recall that the naming convention is snd_<name>. GameMaker: Studio does not include a built-in sound editor, so you will need to make these from an external program or download some royalty-free assets online. The **Edit Sound** button in the sound resource window is just to open up an external sound editor if you linked one. The first button next to the **Name** box is for loading the sound, the one after that plays and loops it for you, and the third one stops the playback of the sound. You can also adjust the base volume of the sound with the slider.

Once you've loaded your three sounds, you can use them. The first one is for when the enemy dies. This should be run when a bullet hits it, so go to the object for the player's bullet. Upon collision with each enemy object, it should play the sound. To do this, the **main1** tab contains an action called **Play Sound** located under the **Sound** section. It is the first option. Drag it in underneath the previous actions and have it play the enemy death sound once (that means leave the **loop** parameter as `false`). If you wanted to make a sound play continuously (as you might for a soundtrack), you would set the **loop** parameter to `true`. Make sure you did this for when the bullet hits either of the two enemies. Next is the sound for when the player jumps back to the start. This is played upon collision with an enemy, so under each **Collision** event with the enemy inside of the player object, have the designated sound play after the health is decremented but before they jump to start. We will do the third sound (for advancing to the next room) after we have implemented that. Test your game to make sure the right sounds play when you expect them to.

My sounds aren't always playing! How do I fix this?

Make sure that your sounds are set to be played on both collisions in both the bullet and the player. If that doesn't work, perform a clean build with *F7* to test your game again.

Keys and locks and advancing to the next room

One final thing you can do that really makes the game good is to add more levels. So far, you have been experimenting in one room that you can't escape from, even though the game is called *Escape the Dungeon*.

So start with creating a second level. Make sure to put in a player, enemies, walls, and most importantly the health control object. Also, add in your background. When you have finished creating your new room, create two new sprites. One should be a lock, and another should be a key. Once you have created these, create an object for each. Both should be solid. Then, that's it for them. Inside of your player, create a variable inside of your **Create** event called `has_key` and set it to 0. Then, add an event for colliding with the key, and have it assign a value of 1 (meaning true) to that variable. Also, destroy the instance of the key. Next, add a **Collision** event with the lock. Test the variable `has_key` to ensure that it is set to `true` (meaning you have already collected the key). The sound for going to the next room should be played and the player should go to the next room. You already know how to make it play the sound, so put that in.

Next, in order to go to the next room, go to the **main1** tab and drag out the second option under **Rooms**; it's a white rectangle with a green arrow pointing to the right. Now the thing about this one is that it will go to the room that follows the current one on the resource tree. To be sure that it goes to the right one and to not have to worry about the ordering, you can alternatively use the **Different Room** action, which is the white rectangle with a green arrow pointing downwards, and then you just select the room the player should go to via its name.

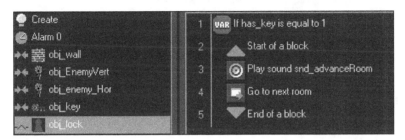

Now, go to your original room and add a key and lock somewhere. Test your game to make sure that it advances to the next room. If you did everything right, then your player should go to the next room if they got the key and hit the lock. Nice job!

Summary

That was one hefty chapter. You learned a lot about GameMaker for just one chapter. Just to review, you learned about movement, collision, timing, sounds, backgrounds, variables, and much more. Did you understand everything? If you were confused about anything, go back and review the content. You can also re-read what you put in your game project or search in the documentation for subjects related to your question. The *Using GameMaker* section of the documentation is helpful for drag and drop programming, which we have used in this chapter. Make sure that you understand everything we did too, at least to a good extent, as we will continue to use the aspects of this chapter and build upon them. This does provide practice, but it is also important to at least understand the basics so you can further advance your knowledge of them. Once you think you've got everything down, tackle these review questions, then the drills.

Review questions

1. What is the difference between the **Keyboard** and **Key Press** event?

2. What is the difference between the **Move Fixed** and **Move Free** actions?

3. What is the difference between regular and precise collision checking?

4. How would you define "steps" in GameMaker? How many steps are there per second? How does this relate to alarms?

5. What are some of GameMaker's built-in variables and what are they commonly used for?

6. What are the four values of direction and which directions are they associated with?

7. What is depth? How is it used?

Quick drills

1. Add narrative to your game by using the **Display Message** action under **Info** in the **main2** tab. You can add a story at the beginning of levels, based on collision events, and so on. Experiment with the display messages to create an engaging story to draw the player into your game.

2. Make a new enemy in your game. Implement the changing sprite based on the direction feature that we had for the other enemies, but put in some kind of new feature so that the previous enemies don't feature. Examples of such features might include providing it a health system, but if you do that, you cannot use the health variable for your enemies and must use a new one because the health variable is global; a new weapon, such as bullets that behave in a new way such as passing through walls; a boss enemy that has multiple attacks, using the event we used before for random shooting; and lots of health.

3. Add a few more levels to your game, each with a lock and key and everything. Then, create a final level in which you have finally escaped the dungeon and have your freedom. Using the **Display Message** action from **Quick Drill 1**, create some kind of winning message to alert the player to their freedom.

4. Add a feature where the player can regain their health, either by pickups or gradual regeneration. Pickups would involve hitting a pickup and getting more health. Regeneration would entail gaining more health every time an alarm goes off. Make sure to cap the health so that the player cannot get too much health. You would cap it by assigning a variable to hold the difference between the total possible health and the current health. If that variable is less than the normal increase, then increment the health by that variable. Otherwise, increment it by the normal amount.

5. This is more of a long drill than a quick drill, but it is an important one. Open up this game's **Global Game Settings**. Under the **Windows** tab at the top, change **Display Name**, **Splash Screen**, and **Game Icon** (you'll need a *.ico and a *.png for the latter two). The splash screen shows up when you launch the game, and the game icon is what appears on the taskbar and in the top left corner of the game window on **Windows** when the game is being run, and the icon that shows up in **File Explorer**. It's possible that these changes won't take effect when compiling your game, depending on whether you are using the Standard Edition or not (Standard will not have the changes take effect). At the side is the **Graphics** tab. It has unfortunately become somewhat of a cliché to use basic windowing in GameMaker rather than using its fullscreen capabilities, which is a shame. To battle this, select the **Start in Fullscreen** mode option. Save your changes there. Now, you will create a standalone application of your game. To do this, go to **File**, then select **Create Application**. The options we recommend are either the **Windows NSIS Installer** or **Single runtime executable**. The first creates an installer to install the game to **Program Files**, and thus the directory you choose here is just for where the installer is located. The second option creates one executable (.exe) file as a standalone file with everything packaged inside (very helpful for rapid testing), and thus the directory you choose here is where the executable will appear. Do either of the two then run your game. Either of these options provides you with the opportunity to distribute a playable version of the game and the end user will not need to have GameMaker: Studio or GameMaker: Player installed in order to play.

6.   Finish editing your game and then save it. Now select **File** at the top left, and then **Export Project**. You can also use the keyboard shortcut *Ctrl + Alt + E* to export it. What this does is, it creates a zipped up version of your work that contains all your assets and everything associated with the project. This is very useful for when you want to work on the project on multiple computers or share it with other people. Save the file you get (a .gmz file) to a flash drive or an online storage service. Find another computer with GameMaker: Studio installed and open up the .gmz file. If you can't find such a computer, just open the .gmz on your current computer. You will find that everything you had been working on will be right there. Use this functionality whenever you need to share your game project or work on it elsewhere, as .gmz files are compressed files of your entire project, and thus take up much less space.

   °   An alternative way to access a project from multiple computers, and perhaps better, is to use source control with a Git, Mercurial, or SVN repository. Google how to set this up, it's pretty easy. Here is the link to a good tutorial on setting up Git https://www.reddit.com/r/gamemaker/wiki/git-gms.

With that, you have completely finished this game in drag and drop programming. Congratulations! It was a lot to create for just one chapter. But you did it. Up next is recreating this entire game in the GameMaker Language and adding some more functionality with that to show what the language can do to extend upon the limitations of drag and drop programming in GameMaker: Studio.

3
Introducing the GameMaker Language

This chapter will introduce you to the GameMaker Language, which is the way that developers who use GameMaker: Studio explore its full possibilities and can directly program their games in a more authentic programming environment. We will focus on GameMaker Language (GML) for the remainder of this book. The previous chapter taught drag and drop programming to provide some familiarity with the GameMaker: Studio environment and provide a base game to model for this chapter. The first chapter taught many different basic aspects of programming in GameMaker, such as input, collision, variables, and more. Few people interested in making advanced games continue to work exclusively in the drag and drop environment, as there are a lot of reasons that the GML is far superior. If you have any experience with the Java or C++ programming languages, it might help, as those taught object-oriented principles, but is definitely not necessary:

- When drag and drop programming is used, the GameMaker compiler must convert it to code, then directly compile it to machine code to be executed. When it does this conversion to code, it is unfortunately not clean and can have excess code that slows your game and makes it act in a way you would not expect. GML gives you direct control over your game so that you are in complete control of what is happening behind it.

- Programming in the GML makes it easier to find and troubleshoot problems as you have directly programmed everything and thus have an easier time understanding how everything is working (or isn't).

- The drag and drop programming environment is very limited and there are many functions that it does not contain, which are vital for the success of a game made in GameMaker. This becomes especially apparent as you really want control over all aspects of your game.

- GML is much more low-level (closer to machine code-like languages such as C or C++, but not so close that you need to write code to long extents) than the drag and drop programming environment. This means you can do more in it and have much more control. Most of the drag and drop functions are high-level, which limits what you could do, in turn limiting your games.

These are a few of the major reasons that GML is superior to drag and drop when it comes to full-scale game development, but there are more, which you might find as you continue to develop games in GameMaker. In the last game, you might have noticed only a few issues that stemmed from working in the drag and drop environment, but when it comes to full-scale games that you will create in GameMaker: Studio, the Game Maker Language is definitely the way to go.

Remaking Escape the Dungeon in the GML

So now that you've heard enough about why to use the GML, let's begin learning it. It will be helpful to open the project from the previous chapter, as we will be copying much of it with edits here and there to make the game better. Open another instance of GameMaker: Studio and create a new project, and name it `escapeTheDungeonGML`. You will need to recreate the resources, but you can retrieve your image and audio assets from the previous game.

Remaking the sprites

Follow these steps for remaking your game's sprites:

1. When you create your new sprite (let's do the player's sprite for now) name it and then select **Load Sprite**. Navigate to `<original Escape the Dungeon root directory>\sprites\images` and you will find all the images of your entire project. It's unfortunately not organized into subfolders, but there shouldn't have been too many sprites in the last project. Select the frontal view we made first in the last chapter.

2. To add your other subimages, select **Edit Sprite** and the familiar old window should open up. Along the top, where the other buttons we have used before are, is a button with a similar function to the white rectangle with the plus logo on it, but instead of a white rectangle with a plus, it is a manila folder with a plus, as you might find in a filing cabinet. This one is two buttons down from the first button we learned, the white *dog-eared* page that adds your image 0 and will load a new subimage from a file (for example, image 1, image 2, image 3, …, and image *n*) into your sprite. You can navigate to the same directory as you did before. When you add these new images, make sure the subimages end up in the same order as in the previous chapter—the front, back, right, and left views. These are the images you replicate for the player.

3. Also, append four more subimages to your player sprite to move to the northeast, southeast, southwest, and northwest in that order. You will have added four more subimages to your sprite, four more that you had not already created. Follow this order as it is easy to remember (it's just a clockwise direction) as shown in the following screenshot:

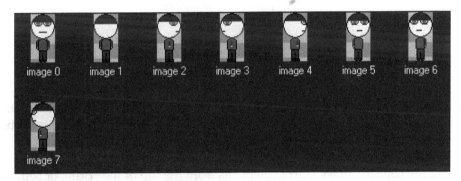

Now, we will modify the collision mask of the player sprite. This is so that we do not have to use precise collision checking (which does have its problems, such as in speed and the fact that it isn't always as precise as we'd like) and so that we don't have the issue of large bounding boxes with regular collision checking. The collision mask is the region of a sprite that another object must hit in order for a collision to be triggered.

4. In order to edit it, select the **Modify Mask** button on the main properties screen for the player sprite. The top right box (labeled as **Bounding Box**) on the left pane is what we care about right now. A screen like the following should appear:

5. In order to modify our collision mask, we must select the **Manual** bullet, which will allow us to edit the four boxes below it. The numbers in the boxes refer to how many pixels in from the related edge the collision mask should start (for example, setting the **Bottom** box to 50 would make the bottom edge of the collision mask start at 50 pixels from the top of the sprite, or setting the **Right** box to 50 would make the right edge of the collision mask start at 50 pixels in from the right side of the sprite). Know that setting collision masks and the numbers you use aren't at all related to the inverted *y* axis in rooms.

6. Set the collision mask so that it starts 2 pixels in from every edge.

The automatic values that are already there before you modify them are not values that make the entire sprite the mask, so make sure that you have the mask begin 2 pixels in from the dimensions of the sprite, not from the values you have already seen before you in the boxes. For example, if your sprite is a 50 x 50 sprite and you want to start your mask 2 pixels in on every edge, your values from left to right and top to bottom would read 2, 48, 2, and 48.

The section labeled **Shape** refers to what shape the collision mask should take. You might think precise is the best, but again, precise can have its issues. Also, most games (not just in GameMaker) have hitboxes (also known as collision masks) based on rectangles, so most of the time you'll probably want to choose the **Rectangle** option.

You might as well get all of your sprites out of the way now, as we don't need to do the sprites and the objects together, step-by-step, when the sprites have already been made. Take a moment to put in all the sprites from the original *Escape the Dungeon* game so you have them available in this version of the game right away. Also, for any other sprites that aren't rectangular (such as for the enemy), or close to it, you might want to modify the collision mask.

Remaking the player object

As always, start making this player object by assigning it a name and a sprite. Also, set it as `solid`. Now, in the previous chapter we had you start with a **Keyboard <Left>** event. But that was a **Drag and Drop** event! Moving forward, we only want to use **Drag and Drop** when necessary! This necessity occurs when the event is simple enough to not cause problems and it would be hard, tedious, or verbose to write in code, *or* when you cannot do the event in code (and there are times that this happens). It will definitely continue to be necessary for setting up properties of your different resources *and* to add four special kinds of events that we will use most often, which we've used before: the **Create**, **Alarm**, **Step**, and **Draw** events!

Understanding the four events

Most of what you do in your games should be handled using these four events, (but do note that there are definitely times when you will need to use others; and these will mainly be under the **Other** or **Asynchronous** sections in the event listing). Become familiar with and understand the four events we listed earlier, as you will use them very often. For events that have multiple types, they are listed in an evaluation order:

- **Create** events: These are run, once, upon the creation of an instance of the object, and are commonly used for variable initialization purposes.

- **Alarm** events: These are used for the timing and they occur once a specified alarm has counted down to 0. Every instance of every object has twelve alarms that can be used.

- **Step** events: These are events inside your objects that are run on every single step. The number of steps per second is defined by your room speed, so a room speed of 30 means that there are 30 steps a second and your **Step** events should be run 30 times every second. Most things are handled in your **Draw** event. There are three different kinds of **Step** events.

    ° **Begin Step**: This is the kind of step event you would choose when you absolutely always need something to run first in an instance in terms of an evaluation order.

    ° **Step**: This is the basic kind of step event that will work for you most of the time. It is run in the middle of the other events.

    ° **End Step**: This is the kind of step event you would choose when you absolutely always need something to run last in an instance in terms of evaluation order.

- **Draw** events: The **Draw** events are what control what is displayed on the screen of your game. Not all drawing requires a **Draw** event; for example, if you are just drawing an object and nothing else, that does not require one, but any special drawing with code must be put in a **Draw** event.

    ° **Draw**: This is the kind of drawing event that will work for many of your drawing needs, and thus, you will mostly need only to use this one. This also has more types:

    Default Draw: This is where you don't even put in a **Draw** event or any drawing-related actions and just an object's sprite is shown, assuming it was set to visible.

    Custom Draw: This is where you will put in a **Draw** event and use drawing-related functions. Unless you tell the object to also draw itself, **Custom Draw** will not draw the object, which is why we put a **Draw Self** action into the game from the first chapter.

    Draw Begin: This is like the **Begin Step** event where it makes sure that something is drawn before the main **Draw** event; again, the event is local to every instance.

    Draw End: This is like the **End Step** event where it makes sure something is drawn after the main **Draw** event; again the event is local to every instance.

- Draw GUI events: GUI stands for graphical user interface, so these events are great for creating a heads-up display to show different important notes to the player, such as their health, lives, ammo, and so on. The **Draw GUI Begin** and **Draw GUI End** functions are similar to the regular **Draw Begin** and **Draw End** events, but they are specifically for the GUI. The **Draw GUI** events are not affected by any changes in view of the room, rescaling, rotation, or anything else and exist on a separate layer of their own, which appears above everything else.

- The other kinds of **Draw** events, while they do exist and are in use, are less important to know, but the ones mentioned here are most important for you to know.

That was one long list of events, but it was an important one. You'll be using all of these events quite often in your game creation.

Starting to code your player object

By now, you should be able to guess that you want to add a regular **Step** event to your player object, so do that. Anytime we want to add a **Step** event rather than **Begin Step** or **End Step**, know that you should add the regular **Step** event:

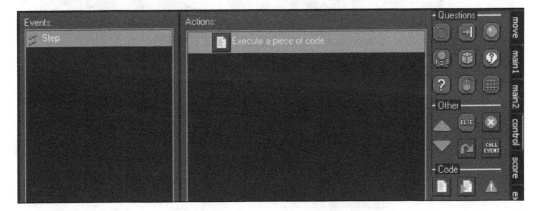

Now, for the rest of the game, there is exactly one action that you will be using, but there are two more that you should know about. They are all located under the **Code** section of the **control** tab. The first action there, called **Execute Code**, allows you to directly put pieces of code directly into the object. The next one is how you call a script via drag and drop and you provide the script name and up to five arguments. If you call a script via code, which is probably the better option, you can supply up to 16 arguments. Scripts are how you can create your own functions in the GML for you to reuse or make code more manageable. We'll learn more about these later. The third action that you see is for putting comments in your drag and drop code, which you might use to leave little notes for yourself rather than regular code commenting, as that is better done in the direct code.

Begin the coding portion of your own game by dragging an **Execute Code** action into your **Create** event. The code editing window will now appear:

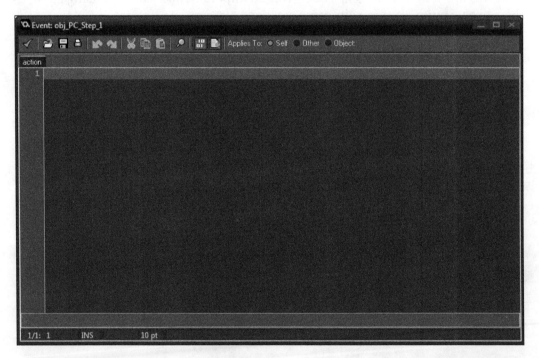

This window is a familiar text editor. The checkmark does the same as usual, as does the **Applies To** section (**Self** means the code is run from the object this code is written in - so in this case self would mean the code is run by obj_PC; **Other** means it's run as though called from an object you are colliding with—but remember that we won't use drag and drop collision events anymore, so we can't really use it; and **Object** means the code will run as though called from every instance of a particular object).

The manila folder with an arrow is to load code from a *.txt file, the floppy disk is to save the code to a *.txt file, and the printer is to print all your code for a hard copy. The arrows are for undo/redo; the following three buttons are for cut, copy, and paste (also usable with *Ctrl + X*, *Ctrl + C*, and *Ctrl + V*, respectively). The magnifying lens opens your **Find** and **Replace** panel, also accessible with *Ctrl + F*, where you can find any text and change it to something else. The same button and keyboard shortcut closes it. You probably don't want to click the following two buttons, as these check your code for errors, which is very helpful.

There is one very nifty feature that you will want to use often when using the **Execute Code** action. You can name (and this name will show up in the **Actions** box in any event in any object) them by typing ///<name> — three forward slashes and any name you want — at the top of your code. For this code block, because we are going to be initializing variables, you should name it Initialize Variables.

Now let's add some actual code here. Set the variable spd to 5. This will be the player's speed.

Making the player move

Close that out, add a **Step** event to your object, and drag an **Execute Code** block into that one. Name the block Movement.

This game example will have the player move in eight different directions — all the points of the compass. In the previous chapter, you started to create your player object by using a **Keyboard <Left>** event. To recreate your keyboard event in GML, you will use the keyboard_check(key) function, where the key parameter is the key whose state (held or not held) you want to check. If you are using a letter, for example, the letter A, then your key parameter would be the value of ord('A'), meaning that you would type in keyboard_check(ord('A')) to check whether the A key is being pressed. When using ord(str), you must always pass a capital letter in single quotes as your str parameter.

The section on **Keyboard Input** is accessible by navigating to **Reference | Mouse, Keyboard and Other Controls | Keyboard Input**, and it is very important that you reference this often, for obvious reasons:

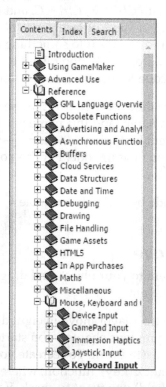

This contains a complete list of all virtual keys, which refer to non-alphanumeric character keys, such as arrow keys, *Shift*, *Esc*, spacebar, and so on. We will first use the virtual key constants for the up and right arrow keys on the keyboard, as northeast (up and right) is the first key combo that we will check for, given that we are putting in eight movement directions. Look at that page in the documentation, and find what the names for the two keys are; **Constant** refers to the parameter that you pass while **Description** is what the key is on the keyboard. You should find that the up key is represented by vk_up and the right key is represented by vk_right, where **vk** stands for **virtual key**. Thus, to check whether the up arrow key is being pressed you would type keyboard_check(vk_up). But of course, it can't be on its own, just as a statement in the middle of your code that evaluates to a Boolean value. Instead, put it inside an if statement, along with a check for the right key, so that it looks like the following:

```
if (keyboard_check(vk_up) && keyboard_check(vk_right)) {
//code
}
```

Typing an `==` `true` here is unnecessary, as not typing it directly implies that you are testing to see if the return value of the function calls is true. Now recall that in the last game, pressing the right key would make the player move right at a speed of 3. When putting code inside this if statement, you won't be using the speed variable. Instead, we will directly modify the x and y coordinates of the player, which is very common to do, and that gives you more control. It also means you don't have to check for a key release with the function `keyboard_check_released(key)`. In terms of making the player move via the use of x and y coordinates, you need to know that decreasing x makes the object move left, increasing it makes it move right, decreasing y makes the object move up, and increasing it makes it move down. Changing the values by 5 pixels in either direction is also common, as is using the shorthand `+=` and `-=` operators. In order for the player to move diagonally up to the right by pressing both the up and right keys, we would want x to be incremented by our `spd` variable (remember, we set that to 5, but we're also using that variable so we can easily adjust the speed later), and y to be decreased by the `spd` variable. The code would look like this:

```
if (keyboard_check(vk_up) && keyboard_check(vk_right)) {
x += spd;
y -= spd;
}
```

The next step is following the same basic code, but substituting other keys for the function. Find all the other arrow key constants you need and test if the specified keys are being held, then act accordingly. Remember to use `+=`, `-=`, and x and y appropriately, depending on the key. You will also want to use `else if` statements for all of the checks, so that you save as much time as possible, since you shouldn't check all of the if statements if you already know the player wants to move in a certain direction. Also, the order of all your `else if` statements should be all the diagonal movements first, followed by the regular up, down, left, and right directions. In this way, the game will make sure that the player doesn't want to move in any of the diagonal directions before testing movements directly on the x and y axis, since the diagonal movements require two keys, but the others require only one, so we should check for the more specific first. Your structure will look something like this:

```
if (keyboard_check(vk_up) && keyboard_check(vk_right)) {
x += spd;
y -= spd;
}
else if (keyboard_check(vk_down) && keyboard_check(vk_right)) {
x += spd;
y += spd;
}
<...>
```

```
else if (keyboard_check(vk_up)) {
y -= spd;
}
else if (keyboard_check(vk_right)) {
x += spd;
}
<...>
```

It is a good habit to save and test your code often. It's especially important to save your code when it works so you have a backup, should something get messed up. The player movement is a great time to demonstrate this importance. As you are coding your movement, you should continually check that the player is moving as you intend, based on your coding. It is much easier to catch and fix an error earlier rather than later. When it comes to troubleshooting code, it is crucial to identify where the code started to fail. In general, if you continually test your program you will notice where the breakdown, from when it is working to when it stops working, exists. When this is the case, you know where the error must be and where to focus your debugging. Even if you cannot find the error on the first release, many games release patches or free DLC, and Valve's Steam distribution system especially has a good system for this. Do make sure, however, that you carefully pick when you are testing, sometimes you'll test at a time that is too early and the code won't work and you'll have to wait until more code has been written.

Changing the subimage

So your movement is working fine, but at this point, you're not really using your character's subimages. To solve this, inside your if statement and all of the else if statements, you will assign a value to the variable image_index, a variable that holds the current subimage of the sprite an object is using. So if an object uses image 3 of its sprite, then image_index will hold a value of 3. Remember what number each subimage corresponded to in your sprite when you assign a value, and also that the subimage values always start at 0 (zero-based indexing). Your code should follow the following format:

```
if (keyboard_check(vk_up) && keyboard_check(vk_right)) {
    x += spd;
    y -= spd;
    image_index = 4;
}
```

Now test your game to see that the correct subimages are displayed and the movement is working fine.

You should notice that your sprite changes as soon as you hit any arrow key but then reverts back to spinning as soon as you stop pressing all keys. To fix this problem, set the value of the variable `image_speed` to 0 in the object's Create Event.

This is a variable that refers to how fast the object cycles through its sprite's subimages, and we used it in the previous chapter whenever we told the player object what subimage to change to. You just didn't realize it. Now the subimage will stay to what it was and never cycle through, and change only when you directly make it change.

Collisions

As of this moment, the player can pass through walls, like a ghost, as we haven't put anything in about collision. Of course, the player shouldn't be a ghost, so we need walls. Make a wall object, assign it a sprite, and flag it as solid. Now, we need to tell the player not to move if it is going to hit one of these walls. Since the player will move by amounts of `spd` pixels, we need to test if there is already a wall where the player wants to move. The `place_free(x, y)` function comes in handy here. It checks whether the instance that calls this function would collide with any *solid* objects if it were at the x and y parameters passed to the function. If there is *no* collision, the function returns a true value (allowing the player to move in our case), and if there is one, it returns a false value (indicating that the player cannot move in our case). You need to, along with making sure the designated keys are being held, ensure that there would be no collision if the player moved (thus meaning you should use the `&&` operator). For moving to the northeast, you would use the `place_free` function to check whether (spd, -spd) relative to the player object is free of solid objects (in this case, the walls, but other objects later on will be set as solid). To do this, you would pass the `place_free` variable parameters of (x + spd, y - spd) within the current if statement as follows:

```
if (keyboard_check(vk_up) && keyboard_check(vk_right) &&
place_free(x + spd, y - spd))
```

In this code, if the up and right keys are pressed, and the place, which is `spd` pixels to the right of the player and `spd` pixels to the north of the player, is free of all solid objects (in this case, currently just walls, but later other objects), then the movement code will be run.

For the regular vertical and horizontal movements, you can just substitute x or y (meaning without modification), respectively. So if the above code didn't check about holding the right key, and it was strictly for moving up, then you could substitute (x, y - spd). Do all this for all of your different if statements. Then put walls inside your room to create another maze. Finally, test your game and make sure that things are working as they should.

Coding the enemies

Your player is working perfectly now, so we can begin work on the enemies. Create one enemy object. Set it as solid so that the player will not walk through them. Inside a **Create** event put in a code block. First, to prevent subimage cycling, set the image_speed to 0. Next, we will use the choose(val0, val1, ..., val15) function, which will randomly select one of its parameters and return that parameter. You do not need to pass it 16 parameters, but you have the option to. The parameter can be a string, integer, variable, or constant:

1. For this game, we will pass the function to two different strings: horizontal and vertical. The return value of the function should be put inside a variable called walk_pattern. Declaring variables in GML, at least for this part right here, can be done simply by typing the variable's name. In GML, we never define a type (such as int, char, and so on), unlike in other languages such as C or C++. Since we want the variable walk_pattern to be equal to the return value of the choose function, we would just type walk_pattern = choose("horizontal", "vertical");. This will also be placed within the code for the **Create** event.

2. You also need to set a variable my_speed (since speed is already a designated variable we need a different name) to hold the value of choose when it has been passed the arguments 2 and -2. For this, add the code my_speed = choose(2,-2);. We will use this variable to decide the initial direction of the enemy after its axis has already been chosen. Finally, set a variable already_set_start to false, and this will be used to test if in our **Step** event; the initial direction of the enemy has already been chosen with my_speed. This will make more sense once you start coding it in the next few paragraphs.

For now, your created event should include the following:

```
image_speed = 0;
walk_pattern = choose("horizontal","vertical");
my_speed = choose(2,-2);
already_set_start = false;
```

Now, you can create your **Step** event. Make two new blocks of code called `Walk Horizontal` and `Walk Vertical`.

Inside the horizontal one, make an `if` statement that tests to see if the variable `walk_pattern` is equal to `"horizontal"`. All of the following code should go inside this `if` statement.

In the previous chapter, the speed variable was used along with direction to make the enemies move. In this chapter, we will not use that variable. Instead, we will use the `hspeed` variable, which refers to the horizontal speed of an object. If it is positive, the object is moving right, and if it is negative, the object is moving left. We can make the enemy move left or right at random, thanks to the `my_speed` variable we set before. Set up an `if`/`else if` construct that first tests whether `my_speed` is equal to 2 and also requires (using the `&&` operator) that the variable `already_set_start` is set to `false` so that the startup direction (left or right) is not set multiple times. You don't need to use `== false`, instead you can put an `!` in front of the variable (such as `!already_set_start`). The `!` is the NOT operator, which would mean here if `already_set_start` is *not* true, then the `if` statement can evaluate to `true`. If this `if` statement evaluates to `true`, then the variable `hspeed` should be set to 2, and the subimage should be set to that of the enemy moving to the right. If the `if` statement evaluated to `false`, then the `else if` should test if `already_set_start` is `false`, and if so, the `hspeed` variable will be set to -2 and the subimage to that of the enemy moving to the left. So far, the code for `Walk Horizontal` should look like this:

```
///Walk Horizontal
if (walk_pattern == "horizontal") {
    if (my_speed == 2 && !already_set_start) {
        hspeed = 2;
        image_index = 2;
    }

    else if (!already_set_start){
        hspeed = -2;
        image_index = 3;
    }

    already_set_start = true;
}
```

The same idea would apply to the code for the vertical movement code, but you will be testing for the string `"vertical"`, using the `vspeed` variable (for vertical speed), and substituting different values for `image_index`.

Test your game. Your enemies should randomly move horizontally and vertically, but you will quickly notice that they are currently going right through the walls.

We will now put in code for when the enemy collides with a wall or another enemy and must reverse its direction and change its subimage accordingly. Outside the `else` (in your horizontal code), put in another `if` statement. Here, we will use the `collision_rectangle(x1,y1,x2,y2,obj,prec,notme)` function to see whether the enemy has collided with a wall, the player, or another enemy. This function will return the ID of the instance collided with, if there is one or the keyword `noone` if there is no collision. Put this function into the `if` statement three times, with an `||` (or) separating each of them so that we can check for a collision with a wall and a collision with another enemy and a collision with the player. Test if the return value is *not* equal to the `noone` keyword by using the `!=` operator. But first, we should break down the parameters:

- The `x1` and `y1` parameters are the coordinates of the top-left corner of the rectangle for which a collision will be checked; `x2` and `y2` are the bottom-right corner of the rectangle.

- `obj` is the object to check for a collision with.

- `prec` refers to if it should use precise collision checking (`true` for precise, `false` for regular), although, as explained before, precise collision checking isn't very good to use.

- `notme` is a Boolean parameter that refers to whether a collision with the instance calling the code either should or should not be checked for. If your `obj` parameter was the same object that the instance calling the code belongs to, but you don't want the calling instance to count for a collision, you set this value to `true`, and if you want a collision with the calling instance to have the ability to occur, or if this is unimportant to you, you can set the value to `false`:

```
if (collision_rectangle(x + <value put for left edge of
bounding box>,
y + <value put for top edge of bounding box>,
x + <value put for right edge of bounding box>,
y + <value put for bottom edge of bounding box>,
obj_wall, false, false) != noone
|| collision_rectangle(x + <value put for left edge of
bounding box>,
 y + <value put for top edge of bounding box>,
 x + <value put for right edge of bounding box>,
 y + <value put for bottom edge of bounding box>,
 obj_enemy, false, true) != noone
|| collision_rectangle(x + <value put for left edge of bounding
box>,
 y + <value put for top edge of bounding box>,
```

```
x + <value put for right edge of bounding box>,
y + <value put for bottom edge of bounding box>,
obj_PC, false, false) != noone
```

You don't have to type it like this; it's just for easier readability. Anyway, let's break all this down:

- We want to use the same bounding box that we gave to our enemy here, so that is why for x1 and y1 you add the value you put for the left and top edges to x and y (respectively), and is also why, for x2 and y2, we add the values we put for the right and bottom edges to x and y (respectively).

- Next, we substitute the objects we want to check for collisions with, so we put in their names.

- The next parameter is whether or not to use precise collision checking, and we don't want to use that, so that should be `false`.

- Finally, the last parameter is the `notme` parameter. Now for the checks for the wall and player, we can set this to `false`, as preventing a check for the enemy calling the code is irrelevant. But for the check for another enemy, we need to set the parameter to `true` (excluding the calling instance), as they would thus automatically always be in that rectangle.

Make sure you called that function three times and separated the three calls by ||
inside your `if` statement.

Inside the curly brackets { }, place an `if`/`else` statement where it tests if `hspeed` equals 2. If so, change the subimage to the one of the left view and make the enemy walk in the opposite direction by typing `hspeed *= -1`, which multiplies `hspeed` by `-1`. Otherwise, the subimage should be set to that of the enemy moving right, and `hspeed` should also be reversed:

```
<if statement from above> {
    if (hspeed == 2) {
        image_index = 3;
        hspeed *= -1;
    }

    else {
        image_index = 2;
        hspeed *= -1;
    }
}
```

Let's break down this code:

- Is the enemy colliding with a wall, another enemy, or the player?
- If so, test whether hspeed equals 2, because, if it equals 2, the enemy is currently moving to the right, and if not it is moving to the left:
    - If it does equal 2, set the subimage to that of the enemy moving left, then reverse the direction so that the enemy moves left
    - Otherwise, set the subimage to that of the enemy moving right, then reverse the direction so that the enemy moves right

Now do the same collision code that you used for your horizontal code, but put it into the vertical code, and of course, still using the vspeed variable instead of hspeed and using different values for image_index.

Test your game five times and watch the direction of two different instances of the enemy.

Did you notice how the axis the enemies travel on and the direction they start off with is always the same (in that, the same instance will always have the same axis and start direction across playthroughs)? This is because the game will always generate the same seed to be used for its randomization functions. This means that every time you play the game, each instance will still have the same return value for the choose function that it had before. So it's not truly random. However, you can make seeds completely random and change across playthroughs by using time. Time is always changing, and thus if you use it to set a seed, your games will always be different.

Random seeds

For this game, and for most other games that you create, you should set the random seed in the creation code (code that is run once a room is created) of a room that is shown before all others that use any random functions. In this way, all of the random functions will be truly random across playthroughs, rather than just random once, and then repeated. To set this up, create a new room called rm_setup and make sure that it is at the top of the **Rooms** section of your resource tree. That way, it will always be the first room to be run. Next, under the **settings** tab is a **Creation code** button. Clicking on it will open the familiar text editor:

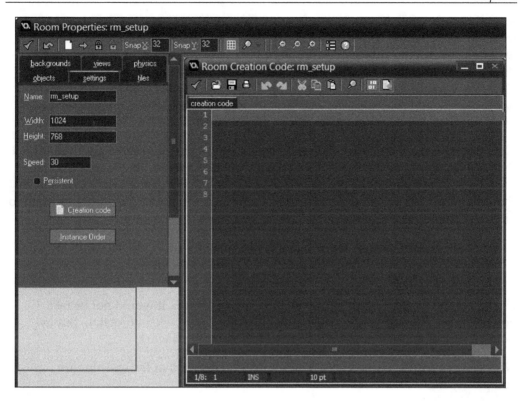

There are three functions we will be using together in order to set a random seed based on time. They are `random_set_seed(val)`, where `val` is what seed you want to be set; `date_get_second_of_year(date)`, where `date` is the date to check; and `date_current_datetime()`. The first function allows you to set the seed, the second allows you to find the second of the year based on the date parameter, and the third tells you the current date. To set these functions up so that you eventually have a completely random seed based on time, type the following into the code editor:

```
random_set_seed(date_get_second_of_year(date_current_datetime()));
```

In this code, the seed will be set to the second of the year based on the current date. Note that the way we are currently doing this isn't always the best practice. Evaluation order can unfortunately vary based on target platform in order to improve optimization. The HTML5 module, for example, might evaluate from right to left rather than left to right as done in Microsoft Windows. It is thus not necessarily good to include many function calls inside of your functions. To solve this, you can set up variables that hold the values of your arguments, and pass these to the function. We also want to use the `var` keyword, which completely sets up local variables that are destroyed once they are no longer needed. These variables are commonly used in scripts and then written off after the script call is complete.

So in this case, we will type `var arg` so that a variable `arg` has been declared local to the room's creation code and will be destroyed when no longer required. Next, we assign the same value as the argument we passed to `random_set_seed` and then pass the variable to the function instead of what we had passed to it before. Thus, the variable will hold a value of `date_get_second_of_year(date_current_datetime())` and the functions would work just the same, and eliminate any problems that you might get from the evaluation order.

Next, you need to tell that room that it needs to go to the main room after having set the random seed. Use the `room_goto(room)` function, where the `room` parameter is the name of the room in the resource tree, you want the game to switch to. Thus, in the end, your seed will have been set and your main room will have been traveled to, all in less than a second. Your code should look like the following:

```
var arg = date_get_second_of_year(date_current_datetime());
random_set_seed(arg);
room_goto(rm_main);
```

If you were to do the setting of the seed in the main room, it would not be fast enough to set the seed before the enemy object uses the `choose` function, but by doing it in a separate room, you've ensured that it will all work.

Now test your game a few times, and you should notice that the enemies are completely random.

Health and lives system

Like in the last game, there is a health system where the player can be damaged if they get hit by an enemy. We need to first set the `health` variable, change it on collision with enemies, and draw its value to the screen via a health bar. We can also put in a lives system, in which when all health is lost, the player loses a life and the room is reset.

So to begin, create a controller object for controlling the health of the player and assign it a depth of `-10` so that anything it draws is not blocked.

Next, you will need to set the variable for `health` to `100` and `lives` to `3`. These are both built-in global variables that GameMaker has. Set them in the room creation code of `rm_setup` so that they are assigned after the seed has been set but before we go to the next room.

We chose to set them up in this room because we want the values to be global across the game, and if we had them set in the **Create** event of the health controlling object, they would reset in every new room, almost like a new game every room. Next, go back to the player and create an **Execute Code** block labeled Damage in the **Step** event. First, use the collision_rectangle function to test if the player has collided with an enemy. Remember to adjust the coordinate parameters so that they match the bounding box of your player. If the player has collided, the health variable should be decremented by whatever value you want it to be decremented by, in our case, the player will have lost 10 health and will be closer to losing a life:

```
if (collision_rectangle(x +  <value put for left edge of bounding
box>, y +  <value put for top edge of bounding box>, x +  <value
put for right edge of bounding box>, y +  <value put for bottom
edge of bounding box>, obj_enemy, false, false) != noone &&
!invincible) {
health -= <value to decrement health by>;
}
```

Now, go back to your object for controlling health. Put in an **Execute Code** block in the **Step** event. If health is less than 1 (as there are times when health won't always be an integer), then the lives variable should be decremented by 1, as the player has lost their health. All of the following code in the health controller object's **Step** event should go inside of this if statement.

You can decrement the lives variable with the -- operator, either by putting it before or after the lives variable. It doesn't matter in this case, but for future reference, putting it first (the predecrement operator) immediately decrements the variable and returns this new value, but putting it after (post-decrement) returns the original value and then decrements the variable. The same applies for the ++ operator, but of course, that is for incrementation by 1. Here's a small code block to further teach about ++ and --. Imagine that the following lines i = 0 are all run in separate programs (so each use of i in each line begins with it having a value of 0):

```
i = 0;
array[i++] = 0; //array[0] = 0, and then i = 1
array[++i] = 0; //i = 1, and then array[1] = 0
array[i--] = 0; //array[0] = 0, and then i = -1;
array[--i] = 0; //i = -1, and then array[-1] = 0 THIS WILL CAUSE
AN ERROR
```

Now that you understand those operators, let's write some more code. If the lives variable is greater than zero (the player still has lives) the health variable should be set back to 100 (as we do not want them to regain all their health if they lost all their lives; this will cause complications later when drawing the health and lives). Then, the player should move to the start position. This is a bit more complex than you might think. Here, we will use the with statement. The with statement is useful for modifying some or many properties of some or many objects, or to have other objects call functions. To use the with statement, you type with (<object name, instance ID number - usually using a variable, or a related keyword>) { //code }. Since we want to modify the player's x and y coordinates, we can provide the with statement with the name of the player object and then use the x and y coordinates as we would normally do. To make them equal to those of the player when they first started, use the xstart and ystart variables.

The following code would be in the step event for the controller object for the health:

```
///Health Depleted
if (health < 1) {
    --lives;
    if (lives > 0) {
        health = 100;
    }
    with (obj_PC) {
        x = xstart;
        y = ystart;
    }
}
```

The health system isn't yet complete, but we will work on displaying the values, and then finish it up, as we have to do some parts of the system in the **Draw** event due to evaluation order of GameMaker events.

Displaying health and lives

So let's display the values of the lives and health variables. First, draw a heart sprite that represents your lives. Make sure that there are a few pixels of whitespace all around the heart; this will aid in spacing out the hearts. Next, we will use a repeat (n) loop to draw one heart for as many lives as the player still has. Use the following code to draw the hearts, which we will then explain. This code should be executed in the **Draw** event for the health controller object:

```
var i = 0;
repeat (lives) {
```

```
        draw_sprite(<name of heart sprite>, 0, 30 + i *
sprite_get_width(<name of heart sprite>) + 4, 34);
        ++i;
}
```

In this code, a local variable i is first set to 0. It is a simple counter variable that represents how many hearts have already been drawn, using zero-based indexing. Next, a repeat loop is run *lives* number of times. The draw_sprite function's first parameter is the sprite to be drawn; the second is the subimage to be used; the third is the x coordinate for the drawing to take place, and the fourth parameter is the y coordinate. To explain the x parameter code, let's walk through each heart. The first heart that is drawn will be drawn at (34, 34), as the variable i is currently 0, which means that the width of the heart sprite received from the sprite_get_width function does not matter for the first heart, and an offset of 4 is added to the original 30. The second heart will be drawn at (34 + *<width of heart sprite>*, 34), as now i has a value of 1 and is multiplied by the width of the heart sprite. The third heart will be drawn at (34 + 2 * *<width of heart sprite>*, 34), as now the variable i has a value of 2, and is again multiplied by the width of the heart sprite. Drawing the lives should be working perfectly now. Test it out to make sure!

Now, we should draw the healthbar. The function for this is draw_healthbar(x1, y1, x2, y2, amount, backcol, mincol, maxcol, direction, showback, showborder). We will explain all of these parameters:

- x1, y1, x2, y2: These are what you would expect the coordinates to use, where the first two are the top-left corner and the last two are the bottom-left corner.

- amount: This is the variable that refers to how much of the healthbar should be filled, and it can have a value between 0 and 100.

- backcol: This is what color the background of the healthbar should be. If you choose to show a background to your healthbar, this is the color that will be shown in depleted parts of the bar.

- mincol: This is the color shown when the value of amount is at its lowest.

- maxcol: This is the color shown when the value of amount is at its highest.

- direction: This is where the bar that shows the value is anchored (which side will be depleted last). It has four values: 0 for left, 1 for right, 2 for top, and 3 for bottom.

- showback: This refers to whether or not the background should be shown, and if it is false then the backcol parameter will be ignored.

- showborder: This refers to whether or not a 1 pixel border should surround the bar's elements (the main bar and the subbar that shows the amount parameter).

So, for your coordinate's parameters, just make the bar appear somewhere in the top-left corner of your room, but make sure that it appears below the hearts for lives. You might need to test your game a few times to get it right. For the amount, we will use the health variable, as this bar is meant for health. You don't always need to use the bar for health though, that's why it lets you choose your variable. You could have it display power, progress, and so on, anything that can be represented by a percent from 0 to 100. As for the color parameters, there are many options that you can use. You can find them all in the documentation by navigating to **Reference | Drawing | Colour and Blending**:

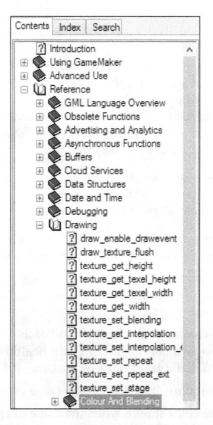

Pick whatever colors you want to use for those parameters. Next, for the `direction` parameter, most healthbars decrease from right to left, meaning the left portion is retained the longest, so in that case you would choose 0. But if you made your healthbar longest on the vertical, you'll want to choose top or bottom. Choose whatever you think looks and works best. As for `showback`, we strongly recommend showing the background, as that is how it can be easily seen how much of the original amount of health there still is, and thus how much you lost. Finally, for `showborder`, this is again your choice.

The drawing part of the health and lives system has been completed, so now we have to go back to finishing up the basic system, which if you recall, we took a break from because we needed to do part of it in the **Draw** event due to evaluation order of events in GameMaker. The next part that we will be doing is where the game will reset if the player has lost all of their lives. To do this, inside of your **Draw** event, put an `if` statement that tests to see if the `lives` variable is less than or equal to 0 (`<=` operator). The reason we include `<` in there is because there is always a chance that GameMaker is somewhat slow or other issues occur. It's a good precaution to include that doesn't hurt at all. The `if` statement here does not need curly brackets, as the code it runs is only one statement, a one-liner, so you can type it directly after the `if` statement's parentheses. `if` statements with one-liners never need curly brackets. Inside of this `if` statement, we will make GameMaker wait a short amount of time, 1 step to be exact, before resetting the game. This is so that the **Draw** event can finish depleting the health bar and draw no hearts so as to properly reflect the respective variables. In order to make GameMaker sleep for a short time, we can use an **Alarm** event. All twelve alarms that every instance of each object has available are held in an array called alarm. As such, to set an alarm and make it start ticking, you can type `alarm[<alarm to set>]` = `<steps to make it count>`. Setting your alarm to have a value greater than 0 makes it tick; setting it to equal 0 triggers it; and setting it to equal `-1` stops it completely from ticking, and at that point it is done.

Remember that we want to make GameMaker wait one step. The alarm that you use does not matter, but we recommend using **Alarm 0** to keep things simple. The code for checking the lives and setting the alarm should be placed at the end of the **Draw** event of the health controller object.

Now, make the event for **Alarm 0**, and inside of it we will display a message and go to the setup room so as to restart the game. The function for showing a message is `show_message(str)`, where str is the string to be displayed. Display a message that tells the player they have lost all their lives and that the game will be reset, then go to the room where the random seed was set with the function `room_goto`, like we used before.

Invincibility

Once you've got all that finished, test your game. You probably noticed that you lose your health really fast. This is because whenever you were up against an enemy, you would lose health. And GameMaker was testing if you were up against an enemy around 30 times a second, so you were losing health around 30 times a second. This is why you would lose all of your health very quickly.

There are a few ways you could fix this. One would be to use an alarm so that you are not continuously damaged. Another would be to make the enemy move away a small amount whenever you hit them. The third one, and the one we will create, is to set up temporary invincibility, where whenever the player hits an enemy, they lose some health (as we already have in place), and then become immune to damage for a short time. After they are no longer immune, they can be damaged again, and then become immune again.

1. To set up this system, first declare a variable called `invincible` inside the **Create** event of your `player` object, and set it to `false`. You can probably figure out what this variable is for.

2. Next, after the player has taken damage from the enemy, the `invincible` variable should be set to `true`, as now the player should be temporarily invincible. Also, in the `if` statement already present there, the `invincible` variable should be set to `false` in order for the whole `if` statement to evaluate to `true` (`&&` operator). Next, set the alarm 0 to 90 steps so that it is triggered after three seconds. This alarm controls how long the player should be invincible. In the **Alarm 0** event, set the `invincible` variable back to `false`, so that the invincibility will expire.

3. The final step is to draw some kind of icon to show that the player is invincible. Typically, the player would flash when invincible, however, that would entail the use of animated sprites. This is not hard, but rather it is something that you will be learning in a later project. First, create a sprite to indicate the player is invincible.

4. Next, add a **Draw** event to the player. Inside of it, use the `draw_self()` function so that both the player and the invincibility sprite can be drawn (as what you are doing is using a **Custom Draw** event, in which the calling object is not drawn by default). The function takes no parameters. If the `invincible` variable is `true` (remember that you still don't need `== true`), then the sprite should be drawn. Also, set the depth of your player object to 10 so that the invincibility sprite will be drawn above everything else.

The icon for invincibility will now appear as long as the player is invincible.

Voilà, you have finished the health and lives system. Play your game a few times and make sure that everything is working perfectly.

Shooting

The next part of your game is to give both the enemy and the player shooting capabilities. First, make the bullet object for your player. If it collides with a wall (collision_rectangle), then it should destroy itself, using the instance_destroy() function (no parameters). Next, declare a local variable (var keyword) equal to the return value of calling collision_rectangle when checking for a collision with the enemy object. The variable will either hold the value noone (no collision with an enemy object) or the instance ID of the enemy object it collided with. Next, test if the variable is not equal to the keyword noone. If there was a collision (meaning that the variable was not equal to noone), then put in a with statement (although you do not need curly brackets for this with statement, as it will be a one-liner) to destroy the enemy. When using the with statement, in between its parentheses should be the variable that you used to hold the enemy's instance ID. After the enemy has been destroyed, the bullet should be too.

1. Next, go to the **Create** event of your player. Inside it, declare the variable can_shoot and set it equal to **true**. Then create an **Execute Code** block in your player's **Step** event. Test to see if the *Shift* key is being held down and if can_shoot equals true. The reason we use the *Shift* key (a modifier key) is due to hardware issues. Some keyboards can have problems with different key combos, such as up arrow + left arrow + spacebar. This is not a GameMaker problem. Gaming keyboards are designed to handle the pressing of many keys at once, but we cannot assume the end user will be using one, so we must plan for the basics, and thus use the *Shift* key. The problem is specifically called "keyboard ghosting", and you can read more about it at https://www.microsoft.com/appliedsciences/antighostingexplained.mspx. You could try using another key (other than *Shift*), but test your game to make sure that you can move and shoot in all eight directions.

2. Anyway, if the *Shift* key is being held down and can_shoot equals true, a local variable should be set equal to the return value of the function instance_create(x, y, obj), as this will store the ID of the instance into the variable. Have the bullet be spawned in the middle of the player.

3. Next, create a with statement and have it refer to the variable you just created. Inside the with statement, the variable direction should be set equal to other.direction. In a with statement, other refers to the main object inside which the with statement is contained. So in this case, the direction of the bullet will be set to the direction of the player. Then, the speed of the bullet should be set to whatever you want it to be set to, within a reasonable amount, for example we set it to 10.

4. Outside of the `with` statement, the variable `can_shoot` should be set as `false` and **Alarm 1** should be set to 30 steps so that the player temporarily cannot shoot. Inside the event for **Alarm 1**, set the `can_shoot` variable back to true so that the player can shoot again.

5. There's one more thing that you'll need to incorporate for the player's shooting. It's somewhat tedious, but it's not hard. In the way that we're currently creating movement, the variable direction does not change. Changing the x and y coordinates does not change direction, so we need to do that manually inside each `if` statement that's for movement. Keep in mind that right is 0, up is 90, left is 180, and down is 270, and from that, figure out the diagonal values (they'll be off by 45 degrees). So under each keyboard check in the **Execute Code** block for movement, set the `direction` variable to a corresponding value.

That was a lot to digest, but the shooting code in the step event for the player should look like this:

```
///Shooting
if (keyboard_check(vk_shift) && can_shoot) {
    var bullet = instance_create(x + <width of player / 2 rounded,
y + <height of player / 2 rounded>, obj_playerBullet);
    with (bullet) {
        direction = other.direction;
        speed = 10;
    }
    can_shoot = false;
    alarm[1] = 30;
}
```

Once you've done all that, test out your game to ensure that the player is shooting correctly and the enemies are being destroyed upon impact with the bullet.

The next part is to get your enemies to shoot. Start with setting up your enemy's bullet. When it hits the wall or the player, it should destroy itself. To make it damage the player, go to the **Execute Code** block in the player we already have for damage. Add a second `if` statement to the code that follows the format of the previous one (even with the same code run if the statement is true), except a collision with the enemy's bullet is checked for and health is decremented by a different amount.

Next, add an **Execute Code** block to the **Step** event of the enemy. We will use the `irandom(n)` function, which returns an integer from 0 to *n* (inclusive of both), and test to see if it returns 0 after having been passed the parameter 19, so that we can have a one-twentieth chance of shooting a bullet. Since 0 is also `false`, you can just put a `!` operator in front of the `irandom` function when calling it. So if the function returns a value of 0, then an instance of the enemy's bullet should be created, and the new bullet's ID should be held in a local variable. Use a `with` statement to assign the new bullet a direction and speed. Remember that `other`, when used in a `with` statement, refers to the instance the `with` statement is inside of. Also, since we did not modify the x and y coordinates directly to move around the enemies, instead we used `hspeed` and `vspeed`, direction is changed automatically by the engine so you do not need to worry about that.

With that, all of the shooting has been completed, so you can test your game to ensure that everything is working right.

Sounds

Since backgrounds are created via the room editor, we need not go over them again, but feel free to add one to your room. We will, however, go over sounds. Create your three sounds—for enemy death, the player getting hit, and when the player moves to the next room (the latter of these will again be put in later). You can load them from `<original Escape the Dungeon root directory>\sound\audio`. Once you've loaded them, let's work on the first sound for when the enemy dies. Find your code for the enemy getting destroyed when the player's bullet hits it. Directly, after the enemy has been hit, we will use the `audio_play_sound(index, priority, loop)` function.

Index is the name of the sound (`snd_enemyDeath` in this case); priority is how important the sound is, that is, a lower priority sound will be dropped in order to play a higher ranking one if the number of sounds currently being played exceeds the limit of 128, or otherwise set by the function `audio_channel_num(num)`, but you need not worry about this second function, nor breaking that limit, at least for now. The priority, of course, does not matter here, especially since we have only three sounds in our game, so you can set that to 0, and we only want the sound to play once (so set `loop` to `false`). Now, use this function twice in your **Execute Code** block for damaging the player, once in each if statement, after **Alarm 0** has been set. You will use a different sound this time to indicate when the player is damaged rather than the sound used for the enemy. We will use the last sound shortly once you set up the lock and key system.

Great! Your sounds should be working perfectly. Test your game to make sure of that and listen to the sweet music of your game.

Keys and locks

This next part is pretty simple. First, create your lock and key objects and assign them sprites. Then, in the **Create** event of your player, set the variable `has_key` to `false`. This will be used to determine whether or not we have a key to open the lock. Next, add an **Execute Code** block to the **Step** event. Hold the value of `collision_rectangle` when checking for a collision with the key into a local variable. If the variable is not equal to `noone`, then the key should be destroyed (using a `with` statement). Then, the `has_key` variable should be set to `true`, as the player has received the key. Next, test whether the player collides with the lock and if they have the key. If both are so, they should go to the next room (so, create that room), and the sound for advancing rooms should be played.

Now, we should have some way to tell the player that they have the key. In the **Draw** event of the player, test whether they have the key, and if so, a symbol that shows this should be displayed in the top-left corner (the `draw_sprite` function).

That's it for keys and locks. Like we said, it's really simple. Test the game to ensure that you can successfully advance to the next room. When you test it, damage yourself in the first room so that you lose one life and a little bit more health. Then, go to the next room, and you should see that the health and lives carried over.

Scripts

This will be a brief tutorial on the use of scripts in GameMaker. Creating a script is like any other resource, and upon its creation, the text editor will open. Notice that in the top right, rather than showing **Self**, **Other**, and **Object**, a small box for changing the name of the script appears. This is because all scripts can be called by anything and thus don't really apply to any specific object. The rest of the text editor is the same, however. Your scripts serve as the equivalent of functions in other languages, meaning that, you create them for reuse or to easily manage things. Your scripts can also have arguments. We're going to set up a simple script that controls the enemy's movements.

Make a new script. Now, open both movement patterns in the enemy object. Cut and paste both of them into this script, and remove the third slashes that you had for naming the code blocks so that, now, it's just `//Walk <Horizontal or Vertical>` depending on the pattern. Also, make the second main `if` statement (the second one that tests whether the horizontal or vertical movement pattern should be used) an `else` statement to reduce redundancy and overchecking, as the enemy can only move horizontally or vertically, at least in this game.

At the top of your script, we must allow it to take in an argument. To do this, we set a variable, axis, equal to `argument 0`. `argument 0` is a keyword that represents the first argument a script can take in. There are `argument 0`, `argument 1`, `argument 2`, ... and `argument 15` available for you to use. This argument that we are using will decide whether the horizontal or vertical movement pattern should be used. Previously, the `walk_pattern` variable was used in the code, but now we are going to replace the use of the variable `walk_pattern` in this script with the use of the variable axis so that we can pass the script the walking pattern.

Once you have finished editing your script, go back to the enemy, and in an **Execute Code** block in the **Step** event, call the script as you would any other function; `<name>(<parameter>);` scripts are really just functions. They are really easy to use and are very helpful, so use them when you can. Test the game out a few times to ensure that you created and called the script correctly.

Summary

So you've finished your text-coded remake of *Escape the Dungeon*. Pat yourself on the back, as like the other chapters, this was a hefty one. Go back and review the chapter so that you properly understand everything. Once you think you've got it down, tackle these review questions, followed by the drills.

You have now successfully finished your first chapter that makes use of the GML. Did you see how great it is and how much you can do with it? Just take a look at the documentation, you'll see that GML opens your possibilities wide open. You can really do a lot with it. In the next chapter, you will learn how to create an endless platformer with infinite spawning.

Review questions

1. Explain what each type of event that we will use is, and what they can be used for.
2. How do you declare a local variable (what keyword do we use)?
3. What are some of the advantages of direct coding over drag and drop?
4. What is a room's creation code and how do you modify it?
5. What is the problem with randomness in GameMaker (think seeds)? And how can you solve that problem?
6. What are some of the "translations" of drag and drop to code that we used?

7. What are the different ways that we have made objects move? Explain them, and think about some of their pros and cons.

8. Review some of the functions we used in this game, not just by rereading this chapter; it might also be good to look at the documentation for even more examples. The documentation is at http://docs.yoyogames.com.

Quick drills

1. If you currently play your game, as long as you are colliding with the enemy, they will flip direction. That doesn't make much sense. Fix this so that they'll only collide when hit head on. You can do this by testing the enemy's hspeed/ vspeed (depending) and using the collision_line(x1,y1,x2,y2,obj,p rec,notme) function, where the only difference from collision_rectangle is that the coordinate parameters are the top and bottom points of the line, not top left and bottom right.

2. See if you can recreate some of the extra things that you did in your game in the previous chapter in code, and for this, you should definitely reference your last game project. If you can't redo them, don't fret, as you might not have learned about the functions necessary yet and not every drag and drop function is directly tied to a GML function.

3. Add ammunition for shooting so that you only have a certain number of bullets. Then, set it up so that you can collect "ammo" packs to provide additional ammo. Of course, you should do this in code. Also, display the ammunition by using the draw_healthbar function, which doesn't just have to be for health.

4. Give the enemies a health system (using a variable hp) and make a small heatlhbar constantly appear above their heads. Make sure to call draw_ self() so that they, along with the healthbar, are drawn.

5. Make a bomb weapon system, where the player can throw a bomb that goes a certain distance before "exploding" (you don't necessarily have to show an explosion, we will teach you about particle systems later) and hurting enemies within a certain radius with the collision_circle(x1, y1, rad, obj, prec, notme) function, where rad is the radius.

6. Add additional temporary "power ups" for your player (for example, speed boost, faster rate of fire, or health and lives boosts, which wouldn't be temporary, of course, and so on).

4
Fun with Infinity and Gravity – An Endless Platformer

The previous two chapters took you through the creation of a dungeon game in which the player moved in all directions of the compass in order to escape a maze-like dungeon in which they were placed. You gave the player the ability to shoot, have health and lives, move to other rooms, and much more, but GameMaker isn't just for top-down or side-scrolling games. You can use it for minigames too, and specifically, in this chapter, we will use it for both platforming and making the game endless until death. GameMaker already contains built-in functionality to do both of these in your projects. There's no real goal in the game except to keep going for the longest time. So without further ado, let's begin to program our game.

Creating an endless platformer

Let's first explain exactly how this game will work. Whenever the player hits a platform, they will bounce into the air, regardless of whether a key was pressed. They will come down in the air too, and bounce on any platforms they land on. Direction can be controlled by the left and right keys. If they do not land again after falling, and thus go off the bottom of the screen, they *die*. As they get higher, the screen will *move*, in that, platforms previously visible and usable will go off screen and disappear. Enemies will be incorporated, followed by the main part of the game—random spawning. The game will finish up with the introduction of menu and message displaying systems.

You can compare this whole game to games such as *Doodle Jump* or *Pixel Jump*.

So let's begin! First, make your player sprite. Give it two subimages, for a left and right view, and modify the collision mask to whatever you think works best for the sprite. Make an object for the player and prevent it from cycling through its subimages. We'll do the rest of the player object in a short while. For now, create a sprite for the platform. Modify its collision mask so that *only the very top of it counts for a collision*. At least, in our case, this was by setting the bottom edge of the mask to 0, which allowed a sliver of the platform to be collided with. We want the player to be able to jump through the bottom, but not fall through the top. Create the object for the platform and flag it as solid.

Great, you're done with the platform, so you can return to the player. In the **Create** event (which you should already have because you stopped the subimages from cycling), set the variable gravity_direction to 270. This variable controls the direction that the gravity is pulling from, meaning that, setting it to 270 (which is down) will cause the force of gravity to pull from below, as if the game were on Earth, or really, any other celestial body. The player won't be pulled to the top or side; rather they will be pulled to the bottom. However, setting this variable *only* alters the gravity's *direction*; it does not set the force of gravity that is done with another variable you will use very shortly.

Bouncing and movement

So once you've got that down, make a **Step** event in your player and, as always, put in an **Execute Code** block. We will use this one to make the player bounce. The player will only bounce if they hit a platform (that's pretty logical but it's always good to plan literally everything out). Once they've hit it, they should go up in the air, at which point (when they are not colliding with a platform) a small amount of gravity should be induced that makes the player begin to move slower into the upward direction until they eventually fall. Also when in the air, the player should be able to move left and right. If the player was in fact colliding with a platform, then there should be no force of gravity acting upon them. Finally, we need to cap the speed that the player can be moving in the downward direction. This is because gravity is cumulative, and it can make the player go *really* fast. GameMaker does not specify a cap on the speed, and as such, the player could move so fast that we don't even see it. Collisions might not even be detected. And above all, that's pretty unrealistic. So a cap is definitely necessary. Now that you understand the structure of what we'll be programming here, let's actually do it:

1. Well first, since the platform is solid and we want to test whether the player is hitting it, we can use the `place_free(x, y)` function we used in the previous chapter to test whether the player is hitting a platform. For the `x` parameter, you can supply the basic `x`, as the player object will be bouncing vertically on the platforms. Next, for your second parameter, pass in `y + 1`. This might seem strange, as `1` is most likely not the height of your player and your player sprite's origin is at the top, but at least in this case it's referring to the bottom of the player plus one pixel down. Okay, so now that you put in the parameters and put the function in your `if` statement, there's one thing to remember. The return value of this function is `false` upon collision, meaning that we need to test whether the function is `false`. So after you've tested for that, the `vspeed` variable should be set to `-10` assuming the `if` statement returns to `true`. In the end, if the player collides with a platform, they will move upwards at a speed of 10 pixels per step (as by definition, any type of speed in GameMaker refers to pixels moved per step).

2. The next part we need to put in is a test to see whether the player is in the air. If so, a small amount of gravity should be introduced, and the player should be able to move left and right. The `if` statement is nearly the same as the last one, except we want to test whether the function is true, not false. If this is `true`, set the `gravity` variable to `0.5`. The player will be pulled with a downward force of 0.5 (gravity is not any sort of standard measure, you just need to see what seems right). Also, inside the `if` statement, we will use a `switch(variable/function call)` statement for keyboard input. There's a good chance you've already used a `switch` statement in other programming projects, but we'll review it anyway. The value you provide is either through a variable, or by calling a function. The `switch` statement will find the value, and then test to see what case you put it in matches with, if any. Switches are to reduce verbosity when testing for many values of one variable or function with the same parameters. The format is as follows:

```
switch(variable/function call) {
case (<possible value>):
<statements>
break; <this is not required in every case>
case (<possible value)>:
<statements>
break; <this is not required in every case>
default: <optional; for when above cases fail>
<statements>
break; <this is not required in every case>
}
```

3. So for this `switch` statement, we will pass it the `keyboard_key` variable, which holds the value of the key currently being pressed. Our `switch` statement will have two different cases, looking for values of `vk_left` and `vk_right`, as these are the two keys we will use to move the player. In each, change the value of the `hspeed` variable to some variant on 4 (positive or negative, depending on the key being pressed) and change the subimage that the object uses so that it matches the direction. Also put a `break` at the end of each of these cases, as this tells the `switch` statement, "We found what we need – stop looking!". After you've implemented these two cases, put in a `default` case. This will activate when neither the left nor the right keys were pressed. If it is run, the player should stop moving on the horizontal axis, and then the switch should break.

4. So now that you've put in this `switch` statement, let's take a moment to discuss the differences between using this and the former structure we used in the previous chapter – `if` statements. On the plus side for this, it's much more organized and reduces verbosity. Also, you might have noticed that in the previous chapter, one key could "overtake" the other, but the overtaken key could not overtake the key that it was overtaken by (meaning, for instance, pressing left and right would make the player move right, no matter the order you pressed the keys in), which was due to the evaluation order. However, on the negative for the use of a `switch` statement, there seems to be a hardware issue, wherein holding one key, followed by holding a second simultaneously, and then releasing this second key would stop the player from moving at all. For example, if you hold the left key, and then also hold the right, the player will move right (as expected), but then releasing the right key will not make the player move in the left direction again. Another issue is that, if you press the left key (or any key you've mapped that requires constant pressing), and then some other key you haven't mapped to anything, nothing will happen until you release both keys and press the one you need. This is because the variable we used holds the value of the most recent key that was pressed. So yes, it does seem like `switch` statements can have a few big issues with keyboard input, but it's always good to know your options, and perhaps the way you use them won't cause issues, perhaps for other uses of keyboard input that aren't for moving.

5. Well anyway, after you've finished your `switch` statement, put in an `else` statement (completely outside of the previous `if`), so, this `else` will be run if there was, in fact, a collision beneath the player. When this occurs, the `gravity` variable should be set to 0. At the end of this code block, test if the `vpseed` variable is greater than 10 (meaning that the player is falling faster than a speed of 10). If so, `vspeed` should be set back to `10` so as to put in a speed cap.

There you have it, you've completely finished the bounce system on your game. Make a room, but have the dimensions set to 512 long by 768 high. For now, manually place platforms all around the room. Test out your game to make sure everything is working as it should (keeping in mind the aforementioned issues).

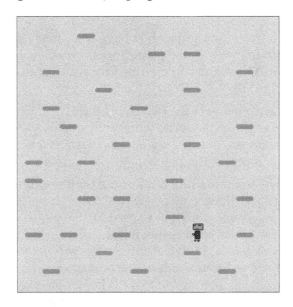

Death and enemies

Okay, so the next thing we're going to incorporate into the game is death, wherein if the player falls off the screen (at its bottom), they will die and the room will restart. This is actually a very simple thing to incorporate. Add another **Execute Code** block below the one you already have to make the player bounce. When the player falls off screen, their y coordinate will be greater than that of the height of the room, meaning that you should test for that. If that if statement evaluates to true, then you should show a message that tells the player they have died and the game will restart (using the show_message function), and then you should restart the room with the room_restart() function. See? Like we told you, it's a really simple system.

After you've put this in, we're going to put in some really quick code that makes the sides of the room loop (meaning that if they (the player) go off the left edge of the screen, they come back on the right, and vice versa). First, test whether the x coordinate of your player is less than 0, meaning that they have gone off the left edge. If so, the value of the x coordinate should be set to the room_width variable, and you can probably figure out what that variable is for. Otherwise, if (else if) the x coordinate of the player is greater than that variable (they have gone off the right edge), then x should be set to 0, which will make them show up on the left edge.

Once you've finished that, test it out in your game to make sure that both features are working great. If so, you can move onto the creation of your enemy. This is a bit more complex than the last part. The way it will work is that, if the player hits the enemy on its bottom, the player will die, but if they hit the enemy on the top, the enemy will die. Follow these steps:

1. First, create your enemy's sprite and object. The enemy sprite should have a smaller width than that of the platform, as this will help in the random spawning later. Make sure you modified the collision mask, and that the object is set as solid.

2. Next, in the **Create** event of the player, set the did_not_hit_enemy variable to true. This variable will dictate whether or not the player has hit the enemy on the bottom. Whenever it is true, they can continue to bounce on platforms, but otherwise they will fall through them.

3. Next, add a new **Execute Code** block to the **Step** event. Test whether the top of the player has hit the enemy object (use the collision_line function), and if so, the player should fall at a speed of 10 (vpseed variable is positive), and the variable we declared earlier in the **Create** event should be set to false, as they now have hit the enemy on the bottom. Finally, there are just a couple of things we need to add to the bouncing code. In the code where you use the place_free function to see whether the player is hitting a solid object, also require that the did_not_hit_enemy variable is true for the if statement to evaluate as true. In this way, they will only bounce if they haven't hit an enemy and *taken damage*. Next, beneath that if statement you just modified, declare a local variable equal to the return value of collision_line when its parameters are for a check for the player hitting the top of the enemy. If this variable is not equal to noone and the player has not hit the enemy on the bottom (use the variable from before), then the enemy should be destroyed (use the with statement). We want it right here, as using the place_free function, like we did, allows the player to bounce on top of enemies, and we need to see whether they hit an enemy and not a platform, and thus whether an enemy should be destroyed.

Well, once you've got all that finished, test your game to make sure that you fall to the bottom of the screen and the room restarts after you hit an enemy, and that they are destroyed if you hit the tops of them. Also make sure that the sides of the game screen loop.

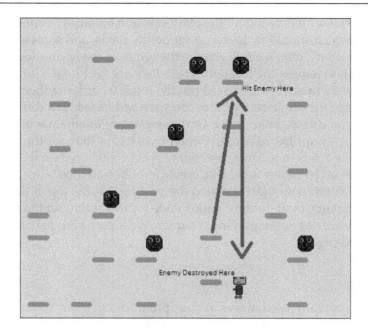

Random spawning

Now, we can finally get to one of the big features of our game—random spawning so that no playthrough is exactly the same.

In this section, we *highly recommend* following all the formats, variable names, and so on. that we provide you, as this will make following along very easy. This section contains lots of tedious and somewhat complex code that, while not difficult, you can get lost in if you don't pay careful attention. On that note, if you used different hspeed and vspeed variables in your player than the ones we provided, change them back, as we use numbers that rely on those speeds. Usually, we give you more control over your projects, but again this is a more complex section.

Let's first plan how we're going to do this random spawning. Four different arrays of objects and coordinates will be set up at the start of the game, as will the random seed. One of these will be an array of the initial pattern of platforms that will always be spawned, and it will be spawned once the main room is created. The other three will be the patterns that are chosen randomly, in that, the game chooses to use one of the patterns and then spawns it, and then chooses another, and spawns it, and so on and so forth. A script will handle the spawning of new platforms. As the player continues to move up, the platforms and enemies will move down and be destroyed when they go off the bottom of the screen.

So let's begin. Start with deleting all the platforms and enemies in your main room except for one, which should be in the center on the *x* axis, and somewhere at the bottom of your room. Next, we will change the origin of the sprites for the enemy and platform. This changes the location where they are anchored. Currently, spawning one of them at (0, 0) would put the top-left corner of them at (0, 0), but we can change the origin so that they are spawned based on a different point. This will make more sense later. In the **Origin** section of the main window for the platform and enemy sprites, select the **Center** button, but then for the platform, set the number in the **Y** box to 0. Thus, the enemy will be anchored on its exact center, and the platform on its center top. Next, create a room called rm_setup, and make sure that it is the first room that is created (by putting it at the top of the **Rooms** section of the resource tree). In the creation code for this room, set the random seed in the same way we did in the previous chapter. We'll now take a short break before beginning to code again.

2D arrays

You've probably already used arrays in your programming, but you might not have used 2D arrays; whereas, the syntax for a one-dimensional array would be:

```
array[0] = 0;
array[1] = 1;
<...>
```

A two dimensional array would have syntax like the following:

```
array[0,0] = 0;
array[0,1] = 1;
array[1,0] = 0;
array[1,1] = 1;
<...>
```

This allows another dimension to exist in your array, as if a regular array has only a length, a two-dimensional array has also a height. You can even create *n*-dimensional arrays, where you just add another subindex. However, while there are functions that check different things about 1D and 2D arrays, not one exists for arrays with dimensions that exceed two, so be careful about using them. We will be using two-dimensional arrays for this project, where each first index is for an object to be spawned as a whole, and the "subindexes" will represent coordinates and the object itself to be spawned.

So let's start setting up an array.

First, we'll make the 2D array call `pattern_initial` that is always spawned at the start, and its indexes and values will follow a format, shown as follows:

```
global.pattern_initial[<val>,2] = <y coordinate>; //spawned    //
first
global.pattern_initial[<val>,1] = <x coordinate>;
global.pattern_initial[<val>,0] = <object>;

global.pattern_initial[<val - 1>,2] = <y coordinate>; //spawned //
next
global.pattern_initial[<val - 1>, 1] = <x coordinate>;
global.pattern_initial[<val - 1>, 0] = <object>;
<...>
```

The `//` that you see indicates a single line comment. Anything after the double forward slash on the line that it is present will not be compiled (and thus not run) by the game. For multiline comments, `/*` (start of block) and `*/` (end of block) are used. Anything between the forward slash and asterisks will not be compiled and run, and the comment blocks can span many lines.

However, for the actual code, `val` represents the number of platforms that will be spawned minus one, as arrays use zero-based indexing, and this initial pattern will spawn only platforms. Also, `global.<variable or array>` will make the variable/array accessible in all of the code in your game. So any object can access the array. The array has what is known as global scope and the same is for variables that are made global. Now, before you begin making your array, you need to know a few things:

- Firstly, assuming that you used the same room dimensions, speeds, values for gravity, and so on that we used earlier in this chapter, the player can only move about 145 pixels left and right when in the air, and 90 pixels up when in the air (we found this out by averaging different distances the player was able to move from point to point). This thus means that all platforms must be within 145 pixels on the x axis and 90 pixels on the y axis of the ones spawned before and after it. This also means that the first platform spawned in this pattern must be within that range in comparison to the single platform you have left in your room, and also that the start and end platforms for the other patterns you will make (the formats for which we will get into soon) must be within the range of *all* other start and end platforms except for the starting platform of the initial pattern.

- The second thing you should know is that you will create your arrays with the first main index you declare being the highest index, and then the first subindex will also be the highest subindex, as this helps for memory allocation as the computer will then know how much memory will need to be allocated. If you were to start from index 0 and then go up, it wouldn't know how much memory is needed, which can cause issues with large arrays. Don't worry if you're confused about all this, we will show you a sample of what your array should look like.

- Also, your *y* coordinate should always be decrementing as you continue to make your array so that there are no gaps or anything.

- Finally, the last platform in this pattern must be spawned very close to the top of your room (very close to 0 on the *y* axis), so you must create enough arrays to make that happen.

The following is a commented sample of what we have:

```
//we have a single platform in main room at (256, 736)
//we have eleven platforms spawned
global.pattern_initial[10,2] = 680; //y coordinate, within
//range of 90px
global.pattern_initial[10,1] = 350; //x coordinate, within
//range of 145px
global.pattern_initial[10,0] = obj_platform; //object to spawn
global.pattern_initial[9,2] = 620; //notice how main index is
//one less from the previous, but the subindex is the same
global.pattern_initial[9,1] = 280; //also note how the y
//coordinate decreased (moving up)
global.pattern_initial[9,0] = obj_platform;
```

So based on this code, you should be able to figure out what your arrays will look like and how you should structure them. Reference this sample when needed, as the spawning method we are using is, while a very good one to use as it prevents the possibility of impossible patterns can be somewhat complex to set up. When you have finished creating your array, make the setup room change to the main room.

Inside the creation code for the main room, we will put in code that spawns this array, using a `for` loop (the structure and syntax of which we will explain now).

The basic format for a `for` loop is:

```
for(assignment; condition; assignment/variable change) {}
```

Usually, the variable you assigned first is a counter variable. The first assignment only happens once, whereas the second occurs after every time that the loop body runs. This second assignment is usually an incrementation or decrementation of your counter variable. The condition is the same as with an `if` statement.

However, there can be deviations from the standard structure, in terms of missing parts. You can skip any of the three parts in the parentheses of the loop provided, which you put in the semicolon that delimits its end as usual (except for the second assignment that doesn't get a semicolon no matter what you are doing). However, you must never have a `for` loop with no condition; it will run infinitely. GameMaker doesn't allow you to have loops with no condition though, these will not compile. In general, most language compilers allow loops with any part missing, so be careful.

Back to the loop we will be writing. A local variable will be declared that holds the value of the highest main index of the array. That variable will then be used to access the necessary values for spawning a platform, and then be decremented and the cycle will repeat until all of the array's platforms have been spawned. The code would look as follows:

```
for (var i = array_height_2d(global.pattern_initial) - 1; i > -1;
--i)
    instance_create(global.pattern_initial[i,1],
global.pattern_initial[i,2], global.pattern_initial[i,0]);
```

First, the local variable, a, is declared equal to the length of the array minus one, as the `array_height_2d(2D array)` function returns the actual height of the first index, not using zero-based indexing. Then, the loop will repeat until the variable is equal to `-1`, an index that arrays cannot have. The strict format we used allows us to have the values inside of the array be used as parameters for the `instance_create` function with a `for` loop.

Once you have finished this, open up the platform object. Give it a **Step** event, and inside it, put in code so that when the platform goes off the bottom of the screen, it's destroyed. Then, test whether the player is moving upwards (which you can do by testing `obj_PC.vspeed`, which gives us the value of the `vspeed` variable of the player object, but you should only follow this format when there is a single instance of the object, like with the player), and if so, the platform's speed should be set to the exact opposite of that of the player. Otherwise (the player wasn't moving upwards), the platform should stop moving. This gives the illusion that the player is actually climbing up, but in the reality of the program, the platforms are just moving and the player is staying in one region. Now copy all of this code and put it in the **Step** event of the enemy object. You can alternatively create a script that both objects call, if you so wish.

After you've done this, test your game to ensure that the platforms are being spawned correctly. If so, you can move on.

The next step is creating the arrays for the patterns that will be chosen at random, and then creating and implementing the script that performs this. The format for these arrays is as follows:

```
global.pattern_<num>[<val>,1] = <x coordinate>; //spawned
//first
global.pattern_<num>[<val>,0] = <object>;

global.pattern_<num>[<val - 1>,1] = <x coordinate>; //spawned
//next
global.pattern_<num>[<val - 1>,0] = <object>;
```

You will create three of these arrays, which will be global. For each of them, the *x* coordinates for the platforms must be within 145 pixels of the *platforms* spawned before and after them. The beginning and ending platforms must also be within the range of all other beginning and ending platforms in the randomly chosen arrays and within the last platform that is spawned from the initial array. Make all of your arrays in the creation code for the setup room, after the initial array is made but before the room changes.

Once you've finished that, we will make a script to spawn new platforms. First, we must test whether there is anything near the top of the screen by using the `collision_rectangle` function. Check whether there is no collision in the area formed by the points `(0, 0)` and `(512, 75)`. The object is all, which is a keyword meaning every single object in the room, but make sure to set the `notme` parameter to `false` so that the player will not trigger a collision. If there's no collision (and all of the following code will be placed in the previous `if` statement), then create a `switch` statement that checks the value of the function `irandom_range(n1,n2)`, where n1 is the low end from which an integer will be chosen, and n2 is the high end from which it will be chosen. Pass it the arguments 1 and 3 so that the function can return 1, 2, or 3. Now we will put in three case statements. Set one up for each of the different possible return values, and do not set up a `default` case.

Let's work on the first case. First, we must declare a local variable, a, equal to the height of the array `global.pattern_one`, which we can do by using the `array_height2d(array)` function, and then subtracting 1 so that the variable uses zero-based indexing. Next, declare another local variable called `last_obj_spawned` equal to `instance_create` when it spawns the object at `global.pattern_one[a,0]` at `(global.pattern_one[a,1], 0)` so that we can base the placement of further spawned objects off of the first object.

Remember that the subindex of 1 holds the x coordinate, and the subindex of 0 holds the object. After the object has been created, decrement the original local variable (a) so that we have "moved on" to the next main index. Now, we will put in a `while` loop that continues until that variable is equal to `-1`, as again no array can hold a value at that index. Inside of this `while` loop, create an `if/else` construct that tests to see whether the object referred to by the current index being used by the local variable is the enemy. If so, create an enemy at (`<specified x coordinate>`, `last_obj_spawned - <half of enemy sprite's width>`) so that the enemy will be spawned (at least on the *y* axis) just above the previously spawned platform. If that `if` statement was false, then a local variable called `spawn_dist` should be equal to the return value of `irandom_range` when it can generate a number from 50 to 80. This variable will specify how far north of the previous object spawned (other than any enemy not spawned first in the pattern) a new platform should be created. Now create a platform (but don't directly reference the platform object, instead reference it through the array so that you can create other kinds of platforms or any other object later on) at the x coordinate specified in the array and the y coordinate of the previous object (`last_obj_spawned.y`) minus `spawn_dist`, so that the platform is spawned at a random (but fair) distance from the previous object, and set the return value equal to the variable we used for what the last object spawned was. After that, decrement the variable we used for the main index, and then break the `case` outside the `while` loop. You can now copy and paste the entire contents of this case, and paste it into the other cases, replacing the references to the array for the first pattern with references to the arrays for the second and third patterns as needed.

When you've finished creating your script, call it at the end of the player object's **Step** event so that new platforms will be constantly spawned. Now play your game and ensure that all the spawning is working as you'd expect it. You might need to tweak some of the x coordinates, but it should be good otherwise.

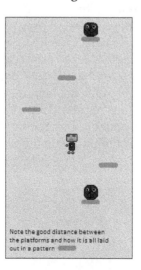

Note the good distance between the platforms and how it is all laid out in a pattern

Menus and textboxes

The last things we will implement into this chapter are menus and textboxes. Menus give us options to perform actions, and the two we will be creating are a menu for a start screen where we can start or quit the game, and one for pausing, where we can resume or quit the game. Textboxes are just boxes of text, as you'd expect, not unlike the boxes that show up with the show_message function.

Menus

We're going to start with creating the menus, and more specifically, the start screen menu. We'll start with the assets we'll need. Begin with creating two sprites. One should be for a **Start** button, and the other for a **Quit** button. Each will have two subimages. The first subimage is for when the button is unselected, and the second is for when it is. We made our buttons 96 by 24 pixels, so you should make yours somewhere around that size. Next, create a font (two options up from **Objects**). Name it what you like, and then select a font on your computer from the drop-down list below the **Name** field. A note about this: fonts are not packaged with the game, which is why we will teach you about another method for fonts that uses sprites, in the next chapter, but there are good reasons to use regular fonts. Anyway, that's all you need to do for the font, so you can now create an object that we will use solely in the start screen. Give it a **Create** event in which the choice variable is set to 0. This variable will be used to hold which button the user has currently selected. Next, add a **Draw** event. Inside of it, we will set the font, the alpha (opacity), and the color to use when drawing the title of the game on the start screen. The functions for this are draw_set_font(font), draw_set_alpha(alpha) and draw_set_color(color). The parameters, respectively, are the font to use, the alpha to use (a real number from 0 to 1), and the color to set for drawing. You must always specify an alpha and color before drawing if you do not use functions in which you specify those values, and must also specify a font if drawing text. Anyway, set those values. Next, we will use the function draw_text_transformed(x, y, string, xscale, yscale, angle), where the string is the text, xscale is the scale you'd like to change the length of the text by (for example, 1 is 100 percent, or regular, 0.5 is 50 percent, or half size), yscale is the same (except for the height), and angle is the angle at which you'd like the text to be aligned (0 is regular, 180 is spun 180°). For the coordinates, you should know that the text is anchored by the top-left corner. Anyway, draw the title somewhere on the screen, and manipulate it however you like.

When you have finished that, we will put in the menu system. First, set the alpha back to 1. Then, make an `if/else` if constructed to test whether the up arrow key has been pressed (the function is `keyboard_check_pressed`), and if not (`else if`), then check whether the down key has been pressed. If the up key was pressed, then the variable `choice` should be set to 0, but it should be set to 1 if the down key was pressed. Now create a `switch` statement for that variable. If it was equal to 0, then use the `draw_sprite` function to draw the second subimage (the one for selected) of the **Start** button, and the first subimage of the **Quit** button. Then, break the case. Do the same for if the variable was equal to 1, but reverse the subimages. In this way, pressing the up or down arrow keys will change the sprite used for the button to let the player know what they are currently choosing. Next, outside the `switch`, test whether the *Enter* key has been pressed. This key is for "pressing" the button. Inside, should be another `switch` for the `choice` variable, with the same cases. If the **Start** button was chosen, then the room should be changed to the setup room. If it was the **Quit** button chosen, then the `game_end()` function should be called, which closes the application. At the end of the **Draw** event, set the drawing color to black. You should always reset your colors and alphas when you're done using them.

Make a start screen room, give it a background, and put the object we just created into the room. Test your game to make sure that the appropriate actions are run when you select and "press" the buttons, and that the sprites change.

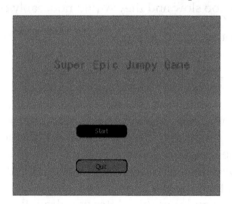

Once it works, we will add a fade out/fade in system. Start off with creating an object to control the transitioning. Give it a really small depth (such as negative one million) so that it will render on top of everything and you don't have to worry about changing numbers or anything. Also, check the **Persistent** checkbox. This will allow it to be created in one room, and then still exist in the next room when the room changes. We have to do this because the fade out part will be in the first room, but the fade in sequence will be in the second room. If we don't make the object persistent, there never will be a fade in.

Next, inside of the object's **Create** event, set a *variable* called `fade_alpha` (not the alpha itself) to `0`, another variable called `state` to `1`, and a third variable called `fade_speed` to `0.05`. The first will be for what alpha we set at different times, the second is to control whether we are fading in or out, and the third controls the rate at which the drawing alpha is changed.

Now, add a **Draw** event. First, set the color to black. Next, we will use the `clamp(val, min, max)` function, which sets a value to something, but ensures that it stays within a range. The first parameter is the basic value to set the return value to, while the second and third create the range that the number will be kept inside. Set the `fade_alpha` variable equal to this function. For the first parameter, use `fade_alpha + (fade_speed * state)`, and for the other two, since an alpha must be within 0 and 1, the parameters should be `0` and `1`. In this way, we will increment (or decrement, based on the value of state) the `fade_alpha` variable by `0.05`. After you have done this, we need to stop the player object from moving up or down when the room is fading out (as we will be using this transition for both going to and from the main room). First, test whether we are fading out (`state` equals 1) and an instance of the player object exists, with the `instance_exists(obj)` function. If so, set `vspeed`, `hspeed`, and `gravity` of the player to 0 (`obj_PC.<var> = 0`). We have to test whether the player exists at all, as we might be fading out from the starting screen (which has no player), not the main room. We must also set these variables here rather than in the player, as doing it in the player would actually be too slow and they would noticeably continue to fall.

After that, check whether the `fade_alpha` variable is equal to 1 (it has hit its maximum value) and if we're still in the first state. If so, go to the room set by the variable `global.target_room` (a variable whose value we will set later). Also, set our `state` to `-1` so that we will start losing alpha. Otherwise, if (`else if`) our `fade_alpha` is 0 and our current state is `-1`, the transition object should be destroyed. Finally, set the alpha to our `fade_alpha` variable, and use the `draw_rectangle(x1, y1, x2, y2, outline)` function to draw our fading transition. The `outline` parameter is whether the rectangle is just an outline (true) or is filled in (false). We want the rectangle to cover the entire screen, so make it filled in. Also, for the second set of coordinate parameters, use the `room_width` and `room_height` variables so as to make this code versatile and reusable. After you draw the rectangle, set the alpha (not the variable, but the direct alpha) back to 1. We found that glitches occurred when transitioning from the start screen to the main room when we did not do this, and it was most likely because we have to pass through the setup room before going to the main one, which is why it's important to set the alpha back to 1.

When you have finished work on your transition object, open the **Creation code** for the setup room. Delete the call to `room_goto`, and replace it by setting `global.target_room` to the main room, followed by creating the transition object. Once that's done, test your game to ensure that you can smoothly transition from the start screen to the main room.

Now let's work on the pause menu. First, create a button sprite just like the others, but for **Resume**. Then, create a new object for the pause menu. Set its depth to `-100`. We'll now start with the **Create** event. Call the function `surface_create(w,h)` with arguments of `surface_get_width(application_surface)` and `surface_get_height(application_surface)` and set it equal to `pause_surface`. The application surface is the default surface everything is drawn on, and we will be basically copying its contents to another surface for reasons we will soon explain. Then, set the variables `is_paused` and `can_proceed` to `false`, and **Alarm 0** to 1 step. Also, set the variable `choice` (used for the same purpose as last time) to `0`. When **Alarm 0** triggers, set that second variable to `true`. We need the surface to exist for a whole step before doing anything more with it, so that it can be created and so that it is registered and everything, which is why we have that second variable and the alarm. Now add a **Step** event, where an `if` statement checks if the `can_proceed` variable is `true` and if the *P* key has been pressed. To use the *P* key with `keyboard_check_pressed`, you simply supply the function `ord('P')`, which returns the unicode value for the key. If the `if` statement evaluated to `true`, then call the `instance_destroy()` function.

Now, we can work on the **Draw** event. First test whether `can_proceed` is `true`. All of the following code will go inside that `if` statement. First, check whether the pause surface exists (as they can get erased on some devices, such as on an Android smartphone if the app is "paused" by an incoming call) with the `surface_exists(surface)` function. If so, draw the pause surface with `draw_surface(surface, x, y)`. You should substitute `(0, 0)` for the coordinates so that the surface covers the whole screen. If the surface did not exist, then use the `event_perform(type, numb)` function to reperform the **Create** event, in which we had drawn the surface and stopped the pause menu from continuing for a step. The type is `ev_create`, and the numb refers to the specific subevent (an example of this would be for a specific key in a keyboard event), which for us will be `0`. After that, test whether the variable `is_paused` is false, which becomes true once all the objects have stopped. If it was false, then it should be set to `true`. Then, use the `surface_set_target(surface)` function to set the surface to draw to be the pause surface. Then, draw the application surface, effectively copying the main surface to the pause surface. Then reset the surface to be the application surface with `surface_reset_target()`. After that, we will deactivate all instances except the pause menu with `instance_deactivate_all(notme)`, where `notme` should be set to `true`. If we set it to `false`, the game would effectively freeze, so it's kind of useless for GameMaker to have the option to set `notme` to `false`, but who knows what people want to do with their games? When we deactivate all the instances, they stop drawing themselves, and thus we see a blank screen. We should see what was there right before we paused the game so that the player doesn't only see the pause menu, which is why we created a surface that holds what the screen used to look like.

After you have finished that, we will put in the menu system that appears when the game is paused. Begin by setting the alpha to a full or somewhat transparent value. Next, we will use the function `draw_roundrect_color(x, y, x1, y1, col1, col2, outline)` to create the background of the pause menu. The `col1` and `col2` parameters are for the center and border colors respectively. Pick whatever colors you want, but set `outline` to `false` (so the rectangle is filled in). After that, you can copy/paste the code we had for the start screen all the way from changing the value of choice based on keyboard input down to the end of the `if` statement that checks for the *Enter* key. There are a few things we'll need to change. First, instead of the first option being the **Start** button, it should be the **Resume** button. You also might need to change some of the coordinates around. Next, if the player "presses" the **Resume** button, the pause menu should be destroyed. If they hit the **Quit** button, set the `global.target_room` variable to the room for the start screen, and spawn an instance of the transition object. In this way, we can have the smooth transition incorporated both to and from the main room. Finally, if you changed the alpha or anything, reset it.

There's just one more thing to add: a **Destroy** event. This is like a **Create** event, but it is run whenever the instance is destroyed instead of when it's created. Inside of this **Destroy** event, call the functions `instance_activate_all()` and `surface_free(surface)`. The first function reactivates all objects in the room (which if you recall, we deactivated in the **Draw** event), and the second deletes the surface (pass it the argument `pause_surface`), as these take up lots of memory and we don't need it anymore until the player pauses again.

When you have completed that, your pause object is finished. The final things to do is to check whether the player pressed the *P* key at the top of the player object's **Step** event, and if so, the pause menu object should be created and should display some text that tells the player that pressing the *P* key pauses the game. Add a **Draw** event to your player object for this. Call `draw_self()` so that the player sprite will be drawn, as will the text. Call `draw_text(x, y, text)` to draw text that tells the player what to press for pausing.

Test out your game to make sure your pause menu is working right and the screen appears paused as well. Also, make sure that both options are working correctly in the menu. If so, we can now work on the final part of this chapter — textboxes!

Textboxes

Congrats! You've made it this far, and have only one thing left to program, a textbox. Unfortunately, GameMaker has no built-in functions for this, which is quite surprising, as most games use a textbox, so we will need to do this on our own. Now, you might say, "What was wrong with the `show_message` function?" A couple things. If you want a game with a nice UI that looks clean, you probably don't want to use that function. It's a dialog box; these are usually for errors or important prompts. Also, that function is for debug purposes, and is not intended for release. In fact, we commonly used it to see the values of variables or to see whether something had ran properly when we were making these games.

So we're going to make a textbox. Unfortunately, you will need to pay very close attention to what we are about to do, as this is actually a rather complex (yet not impossible) and somewhat difficult thing to implement. We will try to explain it as best we can for you to understand, and recommend for this section, as we did with the random spawning, that you use the values we do. So let's start. Make an object for the textbox. Set its depth to -90, so that it renders beneath the pause menu, and give it a **Create** event, in which the variables height and width are set to 128. These will be for the height and width of the textbox. Next, set the variable padding to equal 8. This will be how much blank space there should be from the text to the edges of the box. Now, we get into some of the more complex stuff—**data structure (DS)** lists. These are very similar to one-dimensional arrays; however, they are more dynamic and flexible, and allow us to do more such as shuffle values, change their sorting, or put values in anywhere. That doesn't mean you should abandon arrays, as for one, there are no 2D DS lists, and two, DS lists take up more memory and we don't always need them. Anyway, create a DS list called start by setting the variable start equal to `ds_list_create()`. It will hold the different places at which a new line has been printed (in a number, which is the placement of the character that begins the line). Now set the variables `count`, `last_space`, and `line` to 0. These represent the current spot in the string we will be printing, the place in the message where the last space printed was, and the current line we are printing on. Now set the variable message equal to `global.msg + "#Hit Enter to continue."`, which conjoins the two strings. The # symbol represents a newline. Then, set the variable `str` equal to a completely empty string, and it will be the current line of text that we are printing, whereas the message is the whole string. Now set the variable `global.text_box_finished` to `false`.

Now add a **Destroy** event, and destroy the DS list with `ds_list_destroy(id)`, where `id` should be `start` for us. Add a **Step** event, where you test whether the *Enter* key has been pressed. If so, destroy the textbox and set `global.text_box_finished` to `true`.

1. Now comes the really complex stuff with the **Draw** event. First, set the alpha to whatever you'd like, and draw a round, colored rectangle (using the function we used for the pause menu). Then, set the alpha back to `1`, and set the color to something that is distinctly different from the color you chose for the textbox's background.

2. Now the following order of code might seem strange or unconventional, but it is put in this order so that it will work properly. We start with testing whether `string_width(str)` is greater than `width - (padding * 2)`, as we want to make sure that the lines do that, go out of the box, and that they do leave whitespace around themselves. So if the width of the string is greater, then we must remove part of the original message (just a space) so that it fits. We do this by setting `message` equal to `string_delete(str, index, count)`, where those are all parameters, not any of our variables, and represent the string to modify the position of the first character to get rid of, and how many characters to get rid of. We pass it `message`, `last_space`, and `1`.

3. Then, we use `string_insert(substr, str, index)` and set `message` equal to it. Our parameters (substring to add, string to copy, and position) are the newline character (#), `message`, and `last_space + 1`.

4. Lastly, we use the `ds_list_add(id, val)` function to add `last_space + 1` to the DS list `start`.

5. Now, outside of that `if`, test whether `count` is less than `string_length` when passed a message. If so (there's more to be printed), use `string_char_at(str, index)` to see if it returns the space character when passed `message` and `count`. Outside of this latest `if` statement, (but inside the one where we test the length of the message), increment `count` by 1.

6. We have only a few more things to do in this **Draw** event. Test if the height of `str` is greater than `height - padding` (although you can do `padding * 2` if you find it looks better) with the `string_height(string)` function. If so, increment `line` by 1, as we have gone to the next line.

7. Now, we can actually decide what to print based on all of our calculations. Set str equal to `string_copy(str, index, count)`, which represents the string to copy from, the position to copy from (numbered from 1, not 0), and how many characters to copy. We will pass it `message`, and two calls to `ds_list_find_value(id, pos)`, where the first parameter is the `id` of the list to use, and `pos` is the position to find the value in. In the first call, your DS list is `start`, and your `pos` is `line`. In the second, it's the same parameters, but you will subtract that value from `count`.

8. Finally, draw the message with `draw_text(x, y, string)`, where you should add padding to the object's x and y coordinates, and your string argument should be `str`. Finally, set the color back to black.

With that, there are only a few more things to do, and they are all in the player object. In its **Create** event, set the variable `made_text_box` to `false`. Next, test if that new variable we created in the **Create** event is false. If so, set a variable `global.msg` to a string of text that tells the player they have died and that the game will restart, and then spawn a textbox if so. Spawn it somewhere towards the middle of the screen, not at the top. The reason we must do this is because we made it so that new platforms are spawned if there are no objects (no collision) at the top of the screen, and this object we've just created could cause a collision, thus meaning no new platforms would ever be spawned. Also, inside the `if`, set the new variable we created in the **Create** event to `true`, so that we do not spawn more than one textbox. Finally, test whether `global.text_box_finished` is `true`, and if so, restart the room and delete the call to `show_message`.

Congrats, you've finished the textbox and it it's time to test it out. Make sure that everything works perfectly in your game, and if so, you're done with this chapter.

Applaud yourself. Seriously. It had some difficult stuff. When you're done praising yourself for your hard work, we can move onto the summary.

Summary

Great job on making it this far! You can applaud yourself again if you want. Make sure you review this chapter, especially the part on textboxes and string manipulation, as that can get a little bit confusing. Once you think you're ready, tackle the *Review questions*, followed by the *Quick drills*.

Review questions

1. What's the advantage of the way we "randomly" spawned our platforms and enemies?

2. What does changing the origin of a sprite do for positioning any associated objects?

3. What's a `switch` statement and how is it structured?

4. What are 2D arrays and how do you set them up?

5. How do you create global arrays and variables?

Quick drills

1. Edit the current initial array to include enemies (this is why we had the then-verbose subindex of the platform), and then create another initial array that follows the format of the first. Also put in a script that chooses between the two arrays and then implements the chosen one.

2. Make different messages appear based on different actions in your game. Some might be good to tell the player what buttons to press for different things. A note though, you should make sure that you don't have multiple boxes up at once.

3. Add new items and platforms to your game, such as breakaway platforms (or ones with holes) upon which the player can't bounce, spikes, platforms that move up and down/left and right, or platforms that allow the player to jump for longer. If you can think of any more ideas, try them out!

4. Add power-ups to your game that give the player new abilities, such as ones that make the player fly up for a short time, double jump, increased left and right speed, or any others you can think of.

5. Make some of the values of some of the arrays random values (in a range) to shake the game up even more, but test your game so that you can always keep on going.

With that, you have completed this chapter, so applaud yourself again. Anything you're still confused about, you should definitely go back and read about and maybe you should read about some of the functions in the documentation too. In the next chapter, we will adding more to this game by putting in a score system with a new way to display it, a way to save it as a high score that can be reloaded, and a way to change what the user can enter on their keyboard to make things happen.

5
Saving and Loading Data

In this chapter, you will add a lot of functionality to your previous games. This includes implementing a score system and displaying the score with the use of fancier sprite fonts, saving a highscore to a `.ini` file, which you can then load into your game to show the highscore across playthroughs, as well as allowing the player to change their keyboard configurations for this game, which will then also be saved and loaded. We'll also encrypt the data inside the `.ini` file, after the basics of saving the highscore to it are finished. Using `.ini` files is actually a simple process, as you will see when we get to that part in the chapter.

Putting in a scoring system

For this chapter, you can just work in your previous game and continue to edit that, so you don't need to make any new game projects. Open your infinite platform game, and we'll start with putting in the score system. We will get into drawing and saving it later.

First, add a **Create** event to the platform object. Inside it, set a variable called `hit` to `false`, and it will tell whether or not the player has bounced on it. The player should only be able to score points from a platform once, so that's why we have to put in this variable. Next, below everything you already have in the **Step** event for the platform, test for a collision with the player, and also it is required that the variable we set before is `false`. If so, increment the `score` variable (a built-in global variable) by `10`, and set the `hit` variable to `true`, so that the player can't get more than 10 points per platform:

```
if (collision_line(x + <left edge of bounding box value>, y,
x + <right edge of bounding box value>, y, obj_PC, false, false)
!= noone && !hit) {
    score += 10;
    hit = true;
}
```

Next, we can increment the score whenever an enemy is killed. We'll actually do this in the player's code. In the player object's **Step** event, inside the `if` statement where it tests whether the player hit the enemy on top (it uses a variable) and destroys the enemy (using a `with` statement) if so, increment the score variable by `15` (you will probably need to add curly brackets for this as the previous code was a one-liner).

The final part for just getting the most basic part of the score system to work is to create an object that controls scoring properties. Create a controller object and set its depth to `-90` (as it will draw the score too, later), and then set the variable `score` to `0` in its **Create** event. Put the object into your main room, but don't do it at the top. Somewhere in the middle is probably good, and you should recall why from the previous chapter (the issue with spawning and objects being towards the top of the screen). At this point, while your basic scoring system should be working perfectly, there's no way to display the score, so you can't actually be sure that it's working. To solve this problem, we'll put in a quick rudimentary fix just so you can see everything is working right. Add a **Step** event to the `score` object. Inside, check for a keypress of the spacebar, and if there is one, use the `show_message` function (as this is for debugging and quick-fix purposes, so we don't need to use anything fancy) to display the `score` variable. Once you've put this in, test your game to ensure that the basic score system is working correctly:

```
if (keyboard_check_pressed(vk_space)) show_message(score);
```

If it is, then we can move onto displaying the score. You can start with deleting the **Step** event we just put in the scoring object. The next step is to create our **spritefont**. A spritefont is basically a font, but all the characters are held in subimages of a sprite. All of the subimages must be in ASCII order with no blanks (for example, if you will be printing out . and 0, but not \, you must include \ anyway, either by making a subimage for it with the actual character, or just inserting a blank subimage. The documentation has a page with both ASCII and Unicode (UTF-8) characters and values, located under **Reference | Game Assets | Fonts | font tables**, so you can ensure that you are following the correct ordering and everything. You might also find the website, `http://www.asciitable.com` useful.

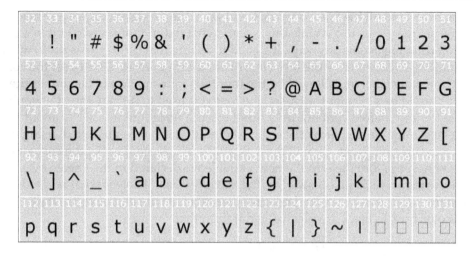

However, for this spritefont, you will need only the numbers 0 through 9. Make a `16 x 16` pixel sprite with 10 subimages. The first subimage must be of the number `0` and the last must be of the number `9` and those in between must go in order. When you have finished creating it, we will set it as a font. In the **Create** event of the scoring object, we will use the `font_add_sprite(spr, first, prop, sep)` function. The parameters are, in order, the sprite in which the font is located, the numerical value of the first character in the font, whether the `font` is proportional (`true`: spacing is based on individual size of characters; `false`: use monospacing based on subimage width), and the spacing to be left between individual characters. For the first parameter, you should know what to do. For the second, you should pass `ord("0")`, as this will give the function for creating the font the numerical value for `"0"`, and this font only contains numbers. As for the last two, we recommend `true` and `4`, as those seemed to look best. Monospacing probably looks best only if all the characters are about the same width, so we advise using proportional fonts most of the time. We also must set a variable equal to the return value of the function, as we have to be able to access and use the font later.

Do that, set the depth of the object to `-90` (so it renders above the player, platforms, enemies, and so on), and add a **Draw** event. This object will be in multiple rooms, the start screen and the main room. This is because when the game is ended, we will want to save the highscore (which we will implement later, when putting in the saving) to a file to be reloaded later. Because it will be in different rooms, and we only want the scores to be displayed in the main room, test if the current room is equal to the main room. The current room is held in the variable `room`, and you just test if that's equal to `<name of main room>`.

If this is `true` (and all the following code will go in the `if` statement we just made), then first set the `alpha` to `1`. While this is somewhat redundant (as we set it to `1` at the end of all drawing events anyway), it's good to ensure that the `alpha` is set to what we want it to, in case there were any bugs or we forgot to reset it. Next, set the color to display the score label in, followed by the font (this font should not be your spritefont, rather it should be a regular font asset, the font you used to display the title would work, as your spritefont contains only numbers and no letters, and we're about to draw a label), and finally, draw the score label so that it can be identified, using the `draw_text` function. Next, we will draw what the actual score is. Set the current font to your new sprite font (held in the new variable we declared in the **Create** event). Now draw the score 50 pixels away on the *x* axis (at least this was what seemed to work for us) from where you drew the score label. At the end of your **Draw** event, set the color back to black, if you changed it from that.

With that, drawing the score is finished, so you should test your game to ensure that it is working correctly. If so, you can move onto implementing and saving a highscore.

Saving and loading a highscore

So in the system we will be implementing, a highscore will be saved to and loaded from an `.ini` file. In terms of the game, whenever the player *dies*, if the highscore is less than the current score, the value of the score will be assigned to the highscore. The highscore, like the regular score, will also be displayed at all times. Whenever the game ends, the highscore will be saved to the `.ini` file so as to reuse it later.

We will save our data using a `.ini` file. While GameMaker contains support for two other methods, text, you can create your own format and parse ASCII characters, and binary, which opens up a file for raw data input (so characters will be represented by their values, not what they are directly, like if you opened it up in a hex editor). INI files are the easiest to start with when beginning to use the GameMaker file system, and using them allows us to teach you a standard format that is very easy to follow. When you're making your own games however, feel free to try your hand at these other functions.

Let's first begin with our `.ini` file. Before we create it, we should go over what it is and its structure. **INI** stands for **initialization**, as these files are commonly used to set up configurations, variables, properties, or other things that can be edited and that need to be constant across uses of a program. These files use sections, properties, and values. You can think of a property as a variable. Comments are denoted by semicolons rather than `//` and `/* */`, not unlike in the assembly language. Some programs might allow for blank lines and whitespace, while others might not, so it is best to have no whitespace just to be sure. Newlines are okay though.

Well enough about that, let's show you how you will make yours. Open up your favorite text editor (Notepad, Notepad++, Atom, Sublime Text, Emacs, Vim, whatever you want). Immediately, select your **Save As** button and save the file as `sav.ini` (sav for save). This might give you some syntax highlighting help in your editor when creating your file. If it doesn't, don't worry, INI files are easy.

In order to declare a section, you type `[<section name>]`. Declare a section named `highscore`. Beneath that, you declare a property just as you would a variable — by typing its name and assigning it a value. Create a property called `highscore` as well, and set its value to `0`, which is the default. You don't need semicolons to end a variable declaration; the end of a line does that. Remember, semicolons denote comments. Also remember that some programs tolerate whitespace, and some don't, so don't include any. Our `sav.ini` file looked like the following:

```
[highscore] ;declare a section called highscore
highscore=0 ;set the default value of highscore to 0
```

Once you've finished up your file, go back to GameMaker. Add a new item to the `Included Files` section of the resource tree. Navigate to the `sav.ini` file and put it in.

Once you've done that, let's put in the highscore system and actually use the file. Open the **Creation** code for your setup room. Put the following code after we set up the arrays but before we transition to the next room. First use the `ini_open(name)` function. The `name` parameter is a string, and is the name of the `ini` file you want to use, including its filename extension. For example, we would type `ini_open("sav. ini");`. After this, declare a variable `global.highscore`. Set it equal to `ini_read_ real(section, key, default)`. The function reads a real number from the `.ini` file that is currently opened, and the first parameter is the section to read the value from, while the second is the property. `key` is synonymous with property. The final is a default value to return if a value was not found in the place we looked, or if there was no `.ini` file at all. It must be a real number, but least for this game, we don't need to worry about it, however a number must still be passed for that parameter. The `section` and `key` parameters are both `highscore` (including quotes, as strings are expected), and your final one can be `0`, but of course you needn't check for that value, as we definitely opened the right `.ini` file that has that section and key. After that, close the `.ini` file with `ini_close()`.

We can now add to our player object the code that changes the highscore if it is less than the score. At the end of the `if` statement, where we test whether the player has gone off screen, test whether `global.highscore` is less than `score`. If so, the highscore should be set to equal the score. In this way, whenever the player dies, the highscore will be updated.

Now open up your score object. Add a **Game end** event, which is under the **Other** section of the events list, shown as follows:

Whenever the game is closed, either through the game_end function or by clicking on the red **X** (at least on Windows), this event will be triggered.

Inside of it, open up our sav.ini file. Then, we will use the function ini_write_real(section, key, value) to save our highscore. The first two parameters are the same as before (with the function that reads a real number), while the third is what value to assign to the property we are writing to. We will write to the section highscore, the key highscore, and the value we write is that of global.highscore. Remember to write your first two parameters as strings with double quotes. After that, close the ini file:

```
ini_write_real("highscore", "highscore", global.highscore);
```

The final part to add is to draw our highscore. In the **Draw** event for this object, directly after we draw the score label, draw a highscore label on the opposite edge of the screen. Then, after the score itself is drawn, draw the highscore.

There's one last thing to do; add this score object to your room for the start screen so that the **Game end** event can trigger when the game is quit via the menu. Usually you would simply flag the object as persistent, but this seemed to cause issues (after we put in the encryption system next) where the **Create** event of the object would not be rerun whenever the main room was reset after the player died, and thus the score would not be reset. You can certainly try persistence, but if your score does not reset after each death, unflag the object as persistent and put it directly into the start screen room, which solved the issue.

Now test your game. You should see that at first, your **Highscore** is **0**, but then, when you accumulate more than that and then die, the highscore is updated, and the process repeats.

When you have finished testing your game, close it out, and open your `sav.ini` file.

Surprised? The value of the **Highscore** key didn't change from **0**! This is because GameMaker isn't modifying the original copy of the file; instead, it's modifying its own copy. On Windows, this copy is located at `%localappdata%\<Project Name>` (and that is an actual directory path you can open in Windows Explorer). If you want to reset your highscore, you can set the value of the key in that file to `0`, or just delete the file completely. When you call the `ini_open` function, if the file you want to open does not exist and you have to read values from it, an `.ini` file will be created, with the name that you specified. The locations for the files on other platforms can be found in the documentation under **Reference | File Handling | File System Limits**, a page which also talks about how GameMaker handles using a filesystem.

Congrats, you're done with your scoring system! The next thing we will do is encrypt our `.ini` file so as to prevent people from cheating.

INI file encryption

Encryption is the process of changing data from a readable form to a more obscure and difficult-to-understand form that prevents people from easily accessing and altering data. And we're going to do it in our games. There are a bunch of ways we could go about this, and since we're not guarding anyone's important credentials, we don't need the most secure methods available such as MIT's new Enigma system or anything like that. The ways you could do it are to use base64 encoding and decoding, or to use mathematical formulas in which you get a number from the highscore, and then convert it to some kind of unreadable string by converting the number to ASCII or Unicode characters, planning for overflow by adding additional characters. Or you could apply bitwise operations (as in the assembly operations AND, OR, or XOR, not those in other programming languages). Other functions exist to check whether a file's values have stayed the same, but these seem to require a web server. For this tutorial, we're going to use base64 encoding.

Now there is one thing you should know about base64. It's a standard. And since it's a standard, anyone dedicated enough to hacking your game could easily decode it. It's recommended that you combine the encode functions with math formulas and other things so that it's not quite as easily hacked. We won't be going over that, as if we did it would kind of make your encryption more easily guessed, but we recommend that you look at some of the math functions and at some ASCII and Unicode tables to figure out an encryption system. There's a lot more than your basic four operators. The top page for the documentation on GameMaker's math-related functions is at **Reference | Maths**. Use the available functions wisely when making your encryption, but get creative.

A useful note though, the bitwise XOR operator (a ^ b) is *very* useful in encryption, and is commonly used, as if you XOR two numbers, and then XOR the result with one of the original numbers, you'll get the other original number as a result. If you don't know what XOR is, it lines up and compares the binary versions of numbers, and every time there is a 1 and a 0, the result will be a 1, but if there is a 1 and a 1 or a 0 and a 0, the result will be 0. So for example, 101110 XORed with 001101 will return 100011.

Let's start with the encryption code, which we will put in the **Game end** event of our score object. Delete what you already have in there, except for opening and closing the .ini file. First declare a local variable (after opening but before closing), which will have held the encrypted version of the highscore. We will use the base64_encode(string) function, which encodes a string in the base64 format, which will be more unreadable to the human eye than a strict number. However, since the highscore is a number and not a string, we must convert the parameter we pass to the base64_encode function to a string using the string(val) function, where the parameter is a real number to convert. In the end, your code should look something like the following:

```
var encoded_highscore = base64_encode(string(global.highscore));
```

You might want to break this up into more variables so as to have code that is versatile no matter the evaluation order, especially if you are planning on distributing to the HTML5 platform.

After that, we will open our sav.ini file and write the string to it with the ini_write_string function, which is the exact same as the ini_write_real function (it even takes the same parameters), except, it expects a string rather than a number for the value parameter. Then close the file.

We will now work on the decryption of the data. In the setup room, delete everything you have related to the `.ini` file except for opening and closing it. Between the code for opening and closing the file, declare a local variable. It will hold the decoded version of the value in the `.ini` file. Use the `base64_decode` and `ini_read_string` functions, which have the same parameters as their counterparts (for encoding and for real numbers), except the latter function takes a string. The decoding function will decode whatever string is in the `.ini` file:

```
var decoded_highscore = base64_decode(ini_read_string("highscore",
"highscore", 0));
```

Finally, set our global highscore variable equal to `real(string)`, when you pass it the local variable we made. This function converts a string to a real number.

There's only one last thing we have to do for this encryption process. First, delete the `.ini` file in `%localappdata%\<Project Name>`. Then change the value of our `highscore` property in the original `.ini` file from `0` to `"0"`, so that it is a string. Finally, delete the `sav.ini` file already in the project from the resource tree, and load the new one.

And you're done with encryption! Run your game and play it a few times. Afterwards, find the copy of `sav.ini` that GameMaker uses, and open it. You should see that your highscore is now saved as a string that you can't exactly decipher on your own. Great! You've implemented a basic system that prevents cheaters from ramping up the score! The final part of this chapter is to give the player customizable control configurations.

Customizable controls

The final system we will be incorporating into our game is one through which players can customize and save their keybinds so that they are different from the left and right arrow keys and the *Enter* key. We will only put in a binding system for these keys, but it is quite easy to extend the system to include other keys, such as the one for pause, and moving the selection up and down on a menu. The keybinds will be saved to our `.ini` file whenever the game is closed, and loaded back in at its very start.

So let's begin putting it in! First, make another button sprite, just like the others that we made, but it will be for modifying the keybindings. When you've finished that, open up the pause menu object. The majority of our code for the keybindings system will be programmed in here, as creating another object could make things complicated.

First, we'll be setting a variable in the **Create** event of our pause menu object. Set binding to false. This is to tell if we are currently rebinding keys (true if so, false if not), and whether keypresses that were already assigned to an action should/ shouldn't perform the action (for example, if we're rebinding, do not modify the choice variable if the up/down arrow keys are pressed, as those keys could have been pressed for a rebind; we won't be rebinding these though, it's just an example).

After you've done that, open the **Draw** event for your pause menu object. Find the code where you change the choice variable to 0 or 1 based on a press of the up or down arrow key. Get rid of that code; the next part is really simple and you'll just start it from scratch. First test whether the up key has been pressed and whether we are not currently rebinding (using the variable we declared in the **Create** event). If so, then put another if statement inside to test whether our current selection (choice variable) is less than or equal to 0 (our choice was the top one, and then we pressed up; and the less than or equal to as there's always a possibility of bugs in GameMaker, and testing for a less than as well doesn't hurt at all). If that second if statement is true, then set our current selection to the last one (give the variable a value of 2). Otherwise, decrement the choice variable. Your if statement should look something like the following, and then you can follow it as a format for your second if statement:

```
if (keyboard_check_pressed(vk_up) && !binding) {
    if (choice <= 0) choice = 2;
    else --choice;
}
```

Outside that if statement we just made, put an else if that tests for a press of the down key and whether we are binding at the moment or not. The code inside of this one is nearly the same as in the other if statement. However, here, you would instead, test whether choice is greater than or equal to 2 (the last option), and set it to 0 (the first option) if so. If it wasn't greater than 2, then increment it so that the selected option moves down one.

The reason we had to put this new system in and take out the old one is because the previous one only worked if you had two options in your menu, but now we have three options, and thus need to make the code more flexible. The old system works perfectly for the start screen, however, as that menu has only two options: **Start** and **Quit**.

The next part is to make the menu background longer (on the *y* axis) so that it can fit three buttons. Once you've done that, we need to draw the third button. Inside of the first switch that we already have there (the one that draws our buttons), draw the button to change the bindings inside of the two cases we already had there, and then add a third case where the button for changing the bindings will appear as *selected*.

At this point, you can test out your game, but just know that your new button won't do anything except get highlighted. Hitting the *Enter* key on it won't do anything at all, but just ensure that you can cycle through all three choices and that they appear *selected* as appropriate.

Now we'll be putting in the rebinding system. Begin with modifying the `if` statement that tests whether the *Enter* key has been pressed. Instead, have it check whether `global.select` has been pressed, as this will hold whatever key we want to use for selecting choices. Also, have this `if` statement make sure that we are not currently binding and that the `just_bound_select` variable is `false`. When we actually put in the rebinding system, the rebinding code will be run before this `switch` statement (so this variable will already be declared), and the key for selecting will also be the last key to be binded. Thus, since GameMaker updates keypresses once per step, at its start, we want to prevent this `if` statement from being triggered just because we rebinded the select key. When this variable is `false`, we have not just rebinded the select key, and when it's `true` we have. It'll make more sense once we put in the actual rebinding part.

Basically, your `if` statement should look something like the following:

```
if (keyboard_check_pressed(global.select) && !binding &&
!just_bound_select) { <...> }
```

Now, inside the `switch` case that this `if` statement runs from, add another case below the ones already there that is for the third possible value of `choice`. Inside it, you should set the variable `binding` to `true`, as we have begun to rebind our keys, and then set the `bound_left, bound_right` and `bound_select` variables to `false`. These three variables tell us whether or not we have rebinded the left, right, and select keys yet (respectively), and at this point, we have not, of course. Also, setting them here, rather than in the **Create** event, allows us to rebind as many times as we want per instance of the pause menu, and will also prevent us from creating more variables that we don't use, because, perhaps, the player opened the pause menu just to pause or to quit rather than rebind. Anyway, after you've assigned these variables, break the case.

The final part to put in is where we actually rebind the keys. Put it right at the beginning of your menu system (right after the `if` statement that tests whether the variable `is_paused` is `false`, which we implemented in the previous chapter). We don't put this code inside the `switch` statement we were just in, as the player won't be pressing all the keys in one step, and the `if` statement that runs the `switch` statement only triggers whether we are not binding, then it starts the binding process if we selected that option and won't be triggered until we stop binding. We'd also need some kind of loop to wait for user input, which is always a bad thing to do, as it will freeze the game. Never use loops for user input.

First, set the `just_bound_select` variable to `false`, as this will be a default value for the variable, which will be set to `true` right after we've rebinded the key for selecting. This also makes sure it goes back to `false`, the step after we finish rebinding. After this, test whether we are currently rebinding. If so (and all of the following code will be put in here), set the font, color, and alpha that we will be using.

Next, we must test whether we have bound the left key yet (`bound_left` will be `false`). If you recall from before, we said that we need a variable to indicate whether the *Enter* key has just been rebinded because GameMaker updates keypresses once per step, at its start. We don't need anything to tell us whether we have just begun binding and whether we should wait a step before rebinding the left key in case it gets assigned to our select key when we first start rebinding, as this code is technically run after we set the variable `binding` to `true` in the `switch` statement at the end of this code. Anyway, inside the `if` statement we just created, to see whether we have not bound the left key, first draw a string of text towards the top of the screen that asks us to press the new keybinding to move left, so that the player knows which key to press. Next, test whether the player has pressed any key, using `vk_anykey`, which represents whether the player presses any key on the keyboard. If so, set `global.left` (the variable that will hold the key for moving left) to `keyboard_lastkey`, which holds the last key that the player pressed. After that, you will have binded the key for moving left, so set `bound_left` to `true`. So far, you'll have something like the following, and you can use it as a model for the following keys:

```
just_bound_select = false;
if (binding) {
        draw_set_font(fnt_title);
        draw_set_color(c_black);
        draw_set_alpha(1);

        if (!bound_left) {
            draw_text(20, 50, "Press the new binding for moving
left.");
            if (keyboard_check_pressed(vk_anykey)) {
                global.left = keyboard_lastkey;
                bound_left = true;
            }
        }
    }
```

Now, create an `else if` that checks whether we have not bound the right key yet (and this should go outside of the `if` statement that tests whether we have bound the left key of course). We want an `else if` so that only one key is binded per step, as GameMaker also only updates which key is being pressed once per step. The code inside here is nearly the same, except the message will ask us to press the new binding for the right key; `global.right` will be set to the last key pressed, and `bound_right` will be set to `true`, as we will have bounded the right key now. After that, create another `else if` statement for the select key. After you set `bound_select` to `true`, set `binding` to `false` (as we are no longer rebinding and `just_bound_select` to `true`, since we have just rebound the select key).

Great job! You've successfully completed rebinding the keys, and the only thing left is to make use of them. You've already implemented it into the pause menu, so there are just three other places to make sure that the correct keys are used. These are the menu on the starting screen, the textbox, and the player. For the first two, replace `vk_enter` with `global.select` (for when choosing menu options and quitting the textbox, respectively) and for the player, replace `vk_left` and `vk_right` with `global.left` and `global.right` (to move left and right in the air in the `switch` statement in the player's code for bouncing and moving). These changes are all in the objects' respective **Step** events.

There's only one thing left to do, you need to set the defaults for these variables. Since right now, we're focused on the basic system and not saving the configurations (that will come soon though), set the global variables that hold the keybinds to the default ones (the key constants) we had used initially inside of the **Creation** code for the start screen room (as this room uses the keybind for selecting a menu option). Otherwise, before you rebind, the things that use these variables won't work and the game will throw you an error log because the variables don't even exist as of yet.

Test your game. Rebind the three keys to whatever you want; just make sure that two of them don't get the same value, and that you don't set a nonrebindable key to a rebindable one (for example, don't set your select key to the up arrow), and then try out the rebind. Rebind a few times and keep trying it out. Once you're sure it's perfect, we'll save these configurations to our `.ini` file.

Saving control configurations

We'll start saving our configurations by modifying our .ini file. Open up the original sav.ini. Give it a section called binds, and give the keys left, right, and select values of 37, 39, and 13, respectively. These are the values of vk_left, vk_right, and vk_enter. We found these out by displaying the values on the screen in a test game. Thus, the default keys will be the arrow keys and the *Enter* key. Remove the .ini file already in %localappdata%\<Project Name>, and remove the included file from GameMaker, replacing it with the new one.

Now create a persistent object for saving the configurations to the .ini file. Add a **Game end** event. Inside of it, open the sav.ini file. Now since keyboard bindings aren't something we need to worry about people hacking (and thus we don't need to encode or decode anything), you can just use the ini_write_real function to save the value of the keybinds to the .ini file. After you've done that, close the .ini file, and place the object in the main room. Its persistence will carry it to the start room if we go there, so that it can save keybinds no matter which room the game ends in.

The final step is to load the binds on game startup. In the **Creation** code for your start menu room, remove the code you have for setting the default binds directly. Instead, open the .ini file, use the ini_read_real function to load in the keybinds to our global keybind variables, and close the .ini file.

Test your game and change the bindings, and make sure that they work. Close your game, and then open the copy of sav.ini that GameMaker uses. You should see that the values for the keys left, right, and select have changed from 37, 39, and 13, and are now all something else. Run your game again to ensure that the new binds are still working. If so, great job! You're done with this chapter.

Summary

Nice job! You finished this entire chapter, and while it was easier than the others, it definitely had some more advanced topics in it. Before you move on to the questions and then the drills, you should definitely review the chapter. Once you feel you're ready to, move on.

Review questions

1. What is an INI file, what are its components called, and how do you structure it?

2. How do you create and use a spritefont?

3. What are the other two ways to use files in GameMaker?

4. What are some different ways that you can encrypt data in GameMaker?

5. What should you combine the use of encoding functions in GameMaker with, and why?

Quick drills

1. Allow the player to rebind other keys that have been used in the game, and save these too.

2. Create a *highscore leaderboard* wherein multiple highscores are saved and ranked.

3. Add score bonus items that the player can pick up.

Nice job! You've now finished the entire chapter, and this game project too! Before moving onto the next chapter, you might want to review the past chapters to ensure that you are comfortable with the functions and so that you have a solid basis in what we've gone over so far. As in any good game, the difficulty ramp will continue to rise as the next chapter increases in complexity. You'll learn about side scrolling platformers (easy), but also views (more difficult), client/server networking for multiplayer, and sprite animation.

Let's get onto scrolling!

6
A Multiplayer Sidescrolling Platformer

In this chapter, you will learn about a few different GameMaker components as you create a sidescrolling platformer game. These include sprite animation, sidescrolling with views, networked client/server multiplayer, and finally, Xbox gamepad support (a section you can safely skip if you don't have an Xbox controller). We've tested all the code on an Xbox 360 Controller, but it should function properly on an Xbox One controller (assuming you have all of your drivers installed). The movement and platforming will be done using an alternate method from what we've used before, which you might prefer and find more efficient. Sprite animation is also very easy, and doesn't really introduce new concepts, but it is important to learn. Networked multiplayer is more complex than other concepts you have learned, but the system is relatively simple enough to use even if you have no prior networking experience. The final, and optional, section on gamepad input allows you to give the player multiple mediums through which they can interact with their game. So what are you waiting for? Let's start the chapter!

Sprite animation

In this section, we will teach you how to animate your sprites as opposed to giving them single subimages for each state that they could be in. This is a very simple concept, so let's dive right in.

For this section, you might want to use an external program for your sprite editing so that you can easily draw different frames of animation for a single state with ease. Most external editors will allow you to (in some way) see the previous frame when editing the next one so that you have a frame of reference. A very good image editor we've found and used (although it is intended mainly for pixel art) is **Aseprite**, which is at http://www.aseprite.org. You could consider it both free and paid, and both versions are the same. For $10, you get a prebuilt program with everything ready, but you can also build the source from Aseprite's official GitHub repository. If you want to build it, some guides are available.

With your image editor, create two different animations, one for walking and one for jumping. Only, ensure that they have the character facing towards the right for each (that is, do not make one animation walk left and one walk right, only do right), as there is a way we can simply reverse the image so that we only need one sprite for two different walking directions. Give the walking animation two frames, but the jumping animation none (you should definitely use these numbers to make following along with the networking section easier later on). To add frames in Aseprite, go to the **Frame** menu and choose **New Frame** (or **New Empty Frame** if you want to start from scratch for the second frame, but that gives you no vantage point). If you are using a different program it will likely be a similar menu item:

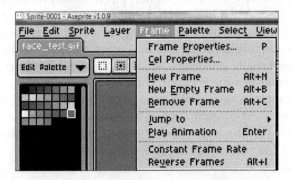

In the end, our two frames for walking looked like the following in Aseprite. It's subtle (notice the positioning of the arms, legs, and eyes), but nonetheless, an animation that's good enough to show that we have animation working in GameMaker:

You can export the animation as a `.gif` file once you're done, as GameMaker: Studio supports GIF importing. You can also export it as a spritesheet, and we'll show you how to import it. Otherwise, you'll probably have to export into separate images.

Spritesheet importing

If you exported the spritesheet, here is how you can import it using the GameMaker sprite editor. Select the **Edit Sprite** option on the sprite's main properties page. Then, select **File** and **Create from Strip**. Load in the spritesheet, and a window, as shown here, should appear:

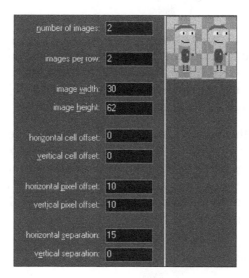

The first three sections should be self explanatory for you, but we'll explain the rest. The offsets refer to the offset of the first image in the spritesheet in terms of number of cells or pixels. A cell would be defined by the width and height of the image. Pixels are easier to use, so we used pixels instead of cells. The separations refer to the separation between each image, in pixels. When you're setting the values for these boxes, you might not end up putting in the values you'd expect, so you'll need to toy around with and tweak the numbers a bit.

Once you have finished making the subimages for your sprite, change the bounding box for it to whatever you think fits. Then, set the origin of both your player sprites to (<half of sprite width>, 0). In this way, the drawing of the player will be anchored on the middle of it. The method we'll use to use this single sprite for drawing both walking directions flips the drawing origin, which can make the shift between walking left and right look very erratic. By centering the origin, the problem is fixed and the flipped sprite appears in the same spot as before rather than across a "mirror" of the sprite direction previously used.

Before we move onto the animation and movement, we'll make a quick platform. Make a sprite and object for a platform, but do not flag it as solid. When you're done with that, we'll go onto movement and animation.

Programming the movement

We'll now move onto the movement, but we're not done with animation. We'll do the animation while we do the movement since both are performed at the same time. Make a player object, and assign its sprite to the *walking* animation sprite via the main properties page.

Now add a **Create** event, inside of which we'll stop the player from animating by setting image_speed to 0. In this tutorial, we won't use idle animations (in fact, do not put one in; otherwise, this will make the networking section a bit harder to follow), but it's basically the same concept as what we will be doing; when the player isn't moving, set its sprite to that of the idle animation.

Once you've assigned this variable, declare two variables called hspd and vspd and set both to 0. In our system, we will not use hspeed and vspeed (so make sure you spelled the variables correctly); rather, we will directly modify the x and y coordinates of our player in a more efficient system. Every time we say "horizontal speed" or "vertical speed" in the following section, pay careful attention that you use the proper variables (our variables, that is).

Now add a **Step** event to your object. We must now put in code that checks whether the player is standing on a platform. We will use the `place_meeting(x, y, obj)` function, which will allow you to test whether a specified object collides with a given point. It returns `true` when there is a collision. Check whether a platform is directly beneath `(x, y + 1)` the player. If so, our `vspd` variable should be set to `0` (since the player should not move vertically anymore). Then, set the `sprite_index` variable to the walking sprite for the player. This variable is like `image_index`, except it holds the sprite being used, rather than the subimage being used. Beneath that, check whether the space button is being held, and if so, set our vertical speed (using our variable, not the built-in one of course) to `-15`, but, you can tweak this variable to your liking later on. Outside, where we check whether a platform was beneath the player, write an `else if` statement to check whether our vertical speed is less than `15` (this will be our max fall speed). If so, increment it by 1 so that eventually, the player will start falling.

After that, we will check whether the left or right arrow keys are being held. If the right key is being held, then set our horizontal speed (again, our own variable `hspd`) to `5`, and if the left key is being held, then set it to `-5`. Neither of these should be `else if` statements, nor should the following statement be. Our final `if` statement will check whether both the left and right arrow keys are being pressed. We needn't check whether both or neither are being pressed, as we redefine our own speed variables at the top of every step. Inside the `if` statement, set both the speed of the image and the horizontal speed of the player to `0`, since they shouldn't be moving when neither or both keys are pressed.

Outside this, just below, will be where the real animation work resides. First, check whether our horizontal speed is greater than `0`. If so (we're moving right), set our current sprite to the walking one, our `image_speed` to `0.5` (so that it is animating), and our `image_xscale` to `1`. This variable is for the horizontal scaling of the sprite being used by the object. A value of `1` (meaning 100 percent) is regular, whereas, a value of `-1` (-100 percent) is completely flipped. It can take other numbered values too. Remember how we made you center the sprite's origin? This variable flips on the origin of the sprite, so by having this origin in the center and not the top-left, we'll see the player flip from facing right to left (and vice versa), but it won't look like it in doing so, they just jumped forward a bunch of pixels. So in the end, the `if` statement checks if we're walking right, and it will make sure that the player object is animating in the right direction if so. The reason we didn't put this up with the key check is because if we did, and then it turned out the `if` statement that checks whether we're pressing both keys got run, the wrong direction might be displayed.

Next, put an `else if` statement that checks whether we're walking left (our horizontal speed will be less than `0`). If so, put in all the same code as the previous `if` statement, except our horizontal scale should be `-1` so that we face left.

Finally, add a regular `if` statement that checks whether our vertical speed is not 0 (meaning, we are either jumping or falling). If so, the current sprite being used should be set to the jumping one. We don't set the horizontal scale, as these are set by left and right movement.

The last part to be added is where we actually make the player move. We'll first work on the horizontal movement part, and it is imperative that you use the order of horizontal code, then vertical code. First, check whether there is a platform with `(x + hspd, y)` pixels to the side of the player. In this way, we can prevent the player from going inside the wall by putting in code that makes them go right next to it.

Inside the `if` statement, put in a `while` statement. Have it verify that there is no platform `(x + sign(hspd), y)` next to us. The `sign(num)` function tells us the sign on the number it is passed. For a negative number, it returns `-1`, for 0 it returns 0, and for a positive number it returns 1. Thus, if our `hspd` variable were to make us move left, we'll check whether there is a platform or wall to the direct left of us. If it would make us move right, we'll check whether there is a platform to the direct right of us. Inside the `while` statement, increment x by `sign(hspd)` so that we move 1 pixel at a time to the left or right and do not go inside a wall. Outside the `while` loop, set our horizontal speed to 0, and outside the `if` statement that this assignment is contained in, increment x by our horizontal speed. Then, after that, set `hspd` to 0 again so that way it will be reset each step for certain. In the end, if moving to the left or right would have put us inside a wall, we will move left or right until we are just up against this wall, and then prevent the player from moving in the same direction anymore. If it wouldn't have, we'll move left or right regularly.

Now you can copy almost all of the code we just wrote (from checking whether moving left or right would put us inside a wall, to incrementing x by our horizontal speed, but not the line after that) and paste it beneath there. Change all uses of x to y, and all references of `hspd` to `vspd`.

After this, you can save and close your player object. Make a room that contains platforms and your player. Make sure that you use some of the platforms as walls and ceilings. Test your game and ensure that you are able to move left and right everywhere, and jump everywhere too. Through our system, you should be able to jump around all you want, change your direction in midair, and be animated when on the ground, like in every platformer you've ever played. Once it's all working, we'll move onto making the platformer actually scroll.

Making your scrolling platformer scroll

This next part is all about view manipulation in your game, and it's actually really easy. It might just be the easiest thing we teach you in this entire book.

So let's get started! We'll first make a background, and then do the rest of this in the room editor. Create a background resource in your project. If you have one ready to import, make sure that it's not the same throughout and that you'll be able to notice differences at different points in the background. Any size should work, as the room editor lets you stretch or loop your background if it's not perfectly fitting to the room size. Of course, when you stretch your background, it loses some quality, so for a game that you publish, you'll most likely want to make a background that fits the room or one that is fit for repeating itself. If you don't have one ready, you can make it with GameMaker directly. The editor for backgrounds is the same as the sprite editor.

After you've made your background, save it and open up your room. Start with the **settings** tab of your room editor. Our `Width` and `Height` were `2048` and `384`, respectively. You should also use these values as this will make the networking section easier later on. By the way, now that we're going to use views, `2048` won't be what's on your screen (in fact, your screen might not even support that), so you can make your rooms as long as you want when using views. Now open the **backgrounds** tab in the editor. Set the room's background to your new background resource with the box right below the **Foreground image** checkbox. If your background doesn't perfectly match the size of your room, you can either have GameMaker loop the background by default, or stretch it by selecting the **Stretch** checkbox as follows:

Once you're done with those things, we'll work on the view manipulation itself. Select the **views** tab, shown as follows:

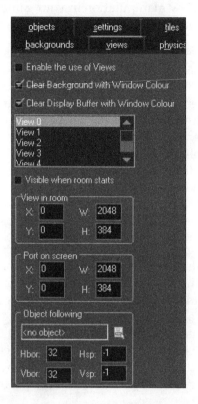

Before we start manipulating the view, let's define what it is. A view is what is displayed on screen, and typically is smaller than the room that the view is of so that you have the ability to show only a portion of the room. For example, if you have a really long and tall room, you'll probably only want to show a portion of it at a time so as to hide things from the player and prevent the player object from appearing very tiny. Now that you know what a view is, we can manipulate it. The first step to follow is to allow GameMaker to use views for this room, which you do by selecting the first checkbox. You can unselect the next two checkboxes, but you should know what they're for, as sometimes you might want them selected.

The first checkbox is about clearing the application surface with the window color. If you know you're going to cover the entire surface, you can leave this unchecked. You'll probably always cover the entire application surface.

The next checkbox is about the backbuffer being filled with a color. You select it only if you know that there will be blank spaces on the screen or if your background has any transparency. The color is black by default, and can be set by `window_set_color(color)`. You don't need to select this checkbox if your views will cover the whole window or if your background fills it.

For our purposes, unselecting these two checkboxes is fine.

Next, make sure that **View 0** is currently selected (in the list towards the top). Make it visible at the start of the room by selecting the checkbox beneath this list. Now we can set the dimensions for the view and its port on the screen (how it's displayed in the window; we'll explain this latter part when we get there). For us, a view width of `512` looked good. As for the height, set it to whatever you like, but `384` (the same height as the room) looked nice for us. Basically, your view will start at `(x, y)`, which will be the top-left corner, and then the bottom-right corner will be defined by your width and height. At this point, you should see a rectangle appear in the room editing side (right side) of your room editor. This is the area that your view will encompass, and thus you can use it to tweak your view values.

The next part is the port on the screen, which is how the view will appear in the game window. If you don't want any stretching at all, give it the same dimensions as your view. But if you do want stretching, smaller numbers in the port will downsize the view, and larger ones will make the view look larger. The `x` and `y` coordinates for your port on the screen should always be `(0, 0)`, anything else will give strange results.

The last part we'll do is the object to follow. By having the view follow an object, it will change based on the position of the object it is following. We want our view to follow the player, so set the object to follow to the player object. Then, the **Hbor** and **Vbor** boxes refer to how many pixels from the edge of the view the object being followed must be for the view to start moving. `80` looked good to us, since you want the player to be able to see some of what's coming up before they reach it. The **Hsp** and **Vsp** are the speeds at which the view will change. `-1` is the default, which means as soon as the player reaches the edge, the view will move as fast as the player. We used `-1` as well for our game.

When you have finished manipulating the view of your game, add more platforms to your room to make it longer and make it truly a scrolling platformer. Once you're done, save your room and run your game. Make sure that the view is set correctly and that it looks right to you. If it looks right, great job! You can move onto client/server multiplayer networking.

Client/server multiplayer networking

This next section will cover multiplayer networking in your game. Note that this is an advanced topic, both in general and in relation to the other topics. But we'll prepare you for it. You'll first have to learn some terms, which we'll explain, so that it won't be hard to understand how what we're doing works when we start writing the code. Without further ado, let's begin!

Networking terminology

Here is some networking terminology to familiarize yourself with before beginning to write your code. There's some more information for each we'll tell you later, but for now you just need to have a basic understanding of these things:

- **Buffer**: This is a region of system memory allocated for you to read and write to, and send in packets/datagrams when used in networking.

- **Packet**: This is the data sent over a network when talking about TCP.

- **Datagram**: This is equivalent to a packet, but for UDP.

- **Transmission Control Protocol (TCP)**: This is a reliable, connection-based networking protocol. It includes error-checking so that all your data is sent, is sent in the right order, and is not corrupted. It being connection-based means that your server and client must be directly connected to each other. The downside is that if you were to, for instance, send `"Hello, World"`, it could be received as `"He"` + `"llo"` + `", Wor"` + `"ld"` rather than `"Hello, World"`.

- **User Datagram Protocol (UDP)**: This is a less reliable, but very useful networking protocol. UDP is faster than TCP, as it does not include as much error-checking, but it does ensure that what is received is what is sent (so if you sent `"Hello, World"` over one datagram, `"Hello, World"` would be received). UDP is not connection-based, rather, it just sends data even if nobody is listening.

- **Socket**: A socket is one end of a TCP connection/UDP session. Multiples of these can exist on a single port (if there are multiple clients). It is what a computer uses to communicate with another computer. Computers do not share sockets. Data is sent over sockets.

- **IP address**: This is a unique address that every device connected to a network has. These are important for a client to be able to connect to a server. IP addresses aren't always known or used by the person, there are also URLs (what you type in your browser's box) that also allow you to connect to a server. The URLs are converted to IP addresses.

- **Port**: A server can communicate on a single port, with clients communicating with the port via their socket. Ports are shared, with a server setting one up and the clients connecting to it (or simply talking to it when talking about UDP). Port numbers are unsigned 16-bit integers, and thus have a range of 0 to 65535.

- **Client/server networking**: Contrary to peer-to-peer networking wherein all computers talk to all the other computers that are connected, this system has a client talk to a server rather than any other clients. The server sends data to and receives data from clients, and is used as a passage to successfully distribute all of your packets. The clients in the end might get data from the other clients, just through a server. Servers are typically run on machines with more processing power, while the client is run on a computer with significantly less processing power. This is true for systems where the server is an external program, and also where the server is included in the same application as the client, but the player must choose to host a server alongside running a client.

Once you've got these terms down, we can move onto having the server find its own IP and display it on a screen, along with its port number.

Printing the server's IP address and port on a screen

The first thing we must do in order to have a client/server system is to have the server display its IP address and port so that players can connect to it. Both are necessary to connect to a server.

The first thing you should do is create a new project in GameMaker. This one will be for the server; as for this game, we're going to have our server in a separate application from the client. Keep in mind however, that you can integrate the server into the same application as your client, we're just doing it this way to keep things a bit more simple and so that we can focus on the networking portion. Converting this example into your own games so that the server is integrated definitely shouldn't be hard.

However, inside the project, create a new object just to find the port. Inside the **Create** event, set the random seed (as we will be generating a random port number to use) in the same way that we set it in previous chapters (such as in the *Random seeds* section in *Chapter 3, Introducing the GameMaker Language*). Then, generate a random number within the range of 49152 to 65535, inclusive, and save it to a global variable called port. That range of port numbers is not preassigned for a specific purpose by the **Internet Assigned Numbers Authority (IANA)**. Thus, it is completely safe to use a port number within that range. Ports can still be taken up in that range by other programs of course, but it is not guaranteed that they will be already taken.

After you've done this, we'll create a UDP server that will be used to find the server's machine's IP address. To do this, use the `network_create_server(type, port, max_client)` function. The first parameter is the type of server we wish to create, and since we want to create a UDP server, we'll use the `network_socket_udp` type. The port should be the port you just created, and for the max amount of allowed clients, you should pass 1, since we only want the server to connect to this. Now, put your function call inside an `if` statement and check whether it returns a value less than 0. A return value less than 0 implies that the function failed when it attempted to create the server. As such, we will show an asynchronous message that tells the user that it failed to create a server for finding the IP address, and asks them whether they want to try again. To display an asynchronous message, we use the `show_question_async(message)` function. Rather than completely freezing the game, an asynchronous function call will allow the game to still run while the message hasn't been interacted with. This function would not be used for debug purposes, whereas the `show_message` function we used before was.

After this `if` statement, put in an `else`, inside which the rest of the **Create** event's code will go. Inside, declare a local variable called `sock` (for socket) equal to the return value of the `network_create_socket(type)` function. Create a UDP socket using the same constant we used earlier, when we made the UDP server.

Next, we will create a buffer. Set the local variable called `buff` to the return value of `buffer_create(size, type alignment)`. The size is how much space should be allocated for the buffer in the system memory, and thus, the maximum amount of data that might be held in it. Our type is `buffer_fixed`. A fixed buffer is one where that size parameter can never change, and the memory allocated will never have to increase. In a fixed buffer, you'll be overwriting data. The byte alignment for us is 1, and you'll see why soon. Byte alignment refers to how many bytes of data the buffer should be aligned to (how many bytes should be used for each number) and it depends on the number of bits that your values might take up and its type. Whenever you read or write to a buffer, it reads, writes, and moves forward by the alignment. For the list of byte alignments in relation to buffer types, in the documentation, go to the page for our `buffer_create` function under **Reference | Buffers**. Scroll down, and you'll see what the alignments should be for different data types and sizes.

See how 8-bit integers should be aligned to 1 byte? This is because 8 bits make up one byte. All 8-bit integers take up a single byte, no more, and so that is why the alignment for an 8-bit integer is 1. Unsigned (positive only) 8-bit numbers go from 0 to 255, whereas the range for signed is -128 to 127. ASCII characters also take up 8-bits, which is why strings are aligned to 1 as well. See the 16-bit number alignment? It is 2, since 16-bits make up 2 bytes, so they need to be aligned to 2 bytes.

Enough about that though, once you've created your buffer and aligned it to 1, we're going to fill it with zeros. 0 is an 8-bit number, so that's why we aligned our buffer to 1. In order to fill a buffer with data, use the `buffer_fill(buffer, offset, type, value, size)` function. The first parameter is the index of our buffer, which you just stored in a variable. Next, is the offset (in bytes) to start at. 0 is the start, so pass the function 0 for our `offset` parameter. The type of data we will fill the buffer with is `buffer_bool`, which can have values of 0 or 1. For the next parameter, we will be filling our buffer with 0, as mentioned before. Finally, the size is how many bytes you want to fill, and our buffer has a size of 32, so pass this function a 32 so that we fill the whole buffer.

After this, we can finally broadcast the buffer with the `network_send_broadcast(socket, port, buffer, size)` function. You already know what to pass the function for the first three parameters. For the `size` parameter, do not pass 32. Instead, pass it the `buffer_get_size(buffer)` function, where you pass this function the index of our buffer. This allows for more versatility.

After this, it is important that we destroy our socket and buffer. Buffers are dynamic resources, such as DS Maps, and they can slow down your program and eventually crash it if you don't get rid of them and keep the space when it's not being used. So, you have to destroy the buffer once you no longer need it. Destroy the socket with `network_destroy(socket)`, and pass it our socket's index. Then, destroy the buffer with `buffer_delete(buffer)`, and again pass the buffer's index.

Once you're done with this, we can add an **Asynchronous** event for the question we asked earlier. **Asynchronous** events are the last section in the **Add Event** dialog, and there are a bunch of different subtypes. We want **Asynchronous Dialog**, as that is what is triggered by a function such as `show_question_async`, so add one. All **Asynchronous** events have a special DS Map available for their duration. It is always called `async_load`, but the keys and values are always different depending on the type of **Asynchronous** event.

At the top of our **Asynchronous Dialog** event, put in an `if` statement. Recall that we can find a value in a DS Map with the function `ds_map_find_value(id, key)`. Put the function inside of your `if` statement. The `id` is the index of the DS Map, and the `key` is a *string* that gives us access to an associated value. The DS Map we want is of course `async_load`, but as for the key, we want `"status"`. That key refers to which button on the dialog the user pressed, and has a value of `true` if they pressed the **Okay** button, or `false` if they hit the **Cancel** button. Check whether they pressed the **Okay** button, and if they did, rerun the **Create** event. Recall that you can do this with the `event_perform(type, numb)` function. Remember our type is `ev_create`, for the **Create** event, and since there are no special sub-events for the **Create** event, give the function 0 for the `numb`. Outside the `if` statement, put an `else`, in which we end the game, since the user didn't want to try again.

Once you're done with that, add an **Asynchronous Networking** event. This will be triggered when the server connects to itself, and we will be able to find the IP address of the machine the server is running on. Inside, make a global variable that will hold the IP address we need. You can get this IP address by loading it in from the special DS Map available to us, and using the key `"ip"`. After this, create an instance of a server object (you haven't yet actually made the object, but just pass the name that you'll give it next), and then destroy the current object.

Great job, you now have the IP address of the machine on which the server runs. We now have to display it along with the port. Make a new object, with the same name as the one you just used in the previous event we were working on. Add a **Create** event for it, and increment our global port variable by 1 if it's less than 65535 (the upper bound of port numbers). Otherwise, if it's greater than 49152 (the lower bound), decrement it by 1. We have to do this because it seemed for us, when we hadn't, the previous port for the UDP server was still being somehow occupied, so we had to change the port to something else for the actual multiplayer server.

Once you've done that, add a **Draw** event to the server object. Set the color and alpha you want to use. Then use `draw_text` to show the server's IP address along and it's port below that. The IP is stored in a string, but the port is a number, so you have to draw the string version of the port with the `string` function. Also, make sure to label the two values (for example, `"SERVER IP ADDRESS: " + global.server_ip`).

At this point, add a room to your game, and put in an instance of the object that find's the server's IP address (the first object). Then run your game, and you should see your IP address and the port number that's being used printed on the screen. If it's working, we can move onto the actual server part of our game.

Creating the actual server

Now go back to your server's **Create** event. Create a TCP server that can have two clients, maximum, and hold its index in a variable. The constant for a TCP server is `network_socket_tcp`. Next, set a variable called `retry` equal to -1. We'll explain its purpose very soon. Then, check whether it failed when we tried to create our TCP server (remember, return value less than 0). If so, set our `retry` variable equal to the return value of `show_question_async`. Have the function tell the user that the program failed to create a server, and ask if they want to try again. Functions that trigger the **Asynchronous Dialog** event will return the index of that function call (so calling the same function twice gives two different values). Usually, when you have an **Asynchronous Dialog** event, you'll have multiple function calls that could trigger it, so you need to figure out which function call triggered it. You use the index of the function call to do this. -1 is an impossible index value, which is why we set the `retry` variable equal to it at first. Later, we will check to see whether this function call triggered an **Asynchronous Dialog** event with this variable.

After you've done this, put in an `if` statement that checks whether `global.` `initialized_server_vars` is `false`, which we'll set an initial value to a little later on. The rest of the **Create** event will go in here. Inside, create an array called `sockets`. It should have two indexes, which should be set to `-1`, since again, these are impossible index values. We're going to store socket indexes here later on. Next, set a variable called `network_array_position` equal to `0`. We'll use this when we have to figure out where in the `sockets` array we should save a socket index.

The final variable we must set is going to be called `data_to_send_buff`. It should hold the index of a buffer, the size of which is `2435` (we'll explain this next) and which is byte aligned to `4`. The reason its size should be `2435` is because that is the maximum amount of data that could be saved in the buffer. It will hold the x coordinate of a player (max of `2048` — make sure your room width is that to make things simpler here), the maximum y coordinate of the player (max of `384` — make sure your room height is that to make things simpler here). It will also hold a `0` or a `1` depending on which sprite that player is using (these aren't the actual indexes — we'll be doing an `if` statement for the two different sprites so it's easier to set a buffer size; if you had an additional sprite, check whether you can combine sprites or simplify your animation to make this networking part easier), a `0` or a `1` for the player's subimage (those are the actual indexes, and if you had more than two subimages in your walking animation, get rid of one to make things simpler), and a `-1` or `1` for the horizontal scaling of the player.

As for the byte alignment of `4`, signed floating point 32-bit numbers take up 4 bytes (signed for horizontal scaling and floating because x and y coordinates can have decimal points). We would have liked to use signed floating point of 16-bit numbers and use an alignment of 2, as that's all the space we need (in fact, it's more, but 8-bit is too small, and you always have to make sure that you use the right bit size for the maximum value for a single number that you might write to a buffer — Google the ranges for the bit sizes if you need help), but at the time of writing, this is not supported in GameMaker. If, however, you're reading this at a time when it is supported (you'll know because the documentation page where you saw the byte alignments to be used won't say floating 16-bit numbers are unsupported), then use a byte alignment of 2 for the buffer in our server and client, and replace all the times we use `buffer_f32` with `buffer_f16`. Otherwise, just do what we're doing if you think that'll be too confusing to follow.

On that note, know that you can have multiple buffers in your games (if, for instance, in one buffer you only have to write a few 8-bit numbers, but in another you need to write some 16-bit integers, you could of course have multiple buffers), but we're just making one because we don't have a ton of data to send in this example and we're making things simple here.

Anyway, once you're done reading all that and making your buffer, set the variable `global.initialized_server_vars` to `true`, since we've set variables in the server that shouldn't be reset. We need to have this check because we might be performing the **Create** event a second, third, or fourth time, and so on, if the server keeps failing to be created (we'll do this in an **Asynchronous Dialog** event soon). We especially don't want to recreate the buffer (that's a lot of wasted memory).

But you might've thought, "Hey, we didn't declare that variable anywhere. We should declare it before testing its value." Good thinking. But were you also thinking we should set it in the **Creation code** for the server room since declaring it in the **Create** event would just reset the variable too and remove its purpose? Unfortunately, you would be wrong to do that, for a really weird reason. GameMaker runs the **Create** events of the objects inside of a room before it runs the **Creation code** of the room. Yes, before a space is even fully created, the things inside of it (or those that could be, since the server object isn't even in the room at the start) are. So we have to do something really redundant to assign the variable a value. Make a new room. In its **Creation code**, set the variable `global.initialized_server_vars` to `false`, and then move to the server room. Make sure the room is run before the server room. Really redundant, right? But unfortunately, there's no other way.

The next part is to make our **Asynchronous Dialog** event. Inside, check whether our `retry` variable equals the index of the function that triggered this event and whether the user pressed **Okay** rather than **Cancel** on the dialog box. The index is stored in the key `"id"`, and recall that to check which button the user pressed, we use the key `"status"`, where pressing **Okay** gives a true value. Inside the `if` statement, show an asynchronous message with the function `show_message_async` that tells the user to try again if the issue persists. Then, perform the **Create** event again.

Outside the `if` statement, put in an `else if` that just checks whether the previous `if` statement didn't run because the user pressed **Cancel** (meaning that `"id"` will still have the index of the `show_question_async` function we called earlier). End the game inside the `else if`. When you're done with that, we'll put in the second last component of the server — the **Asynchronous Networking** event and handling data.

Our Asynchronous Networking event

Yes, this section is so big it even has its own heading. So get ready, and get focused. We won't make it overly difficult or anything, but just know that this part is going to be a bit harder.

So begin with creating an **Asynchronous Networking** event in your server object. Inside, create a `switch` statement. You should have it check what the value of the `"type"` key is of our `async_load` DS Map. We will have three cases.

Connection

The first case should run if the value was `network_type_connect`. Whenever a client connects to the server, the `"type"` key will have this value. Inside of this case, set a local variable called `just_connected_socket` equal to the `"socket"` value of the `async_load` DS Map. We now have the index of the socket of the newly connected client. The `"socket"` key is available only during a connection and disconnection of a client to the server. Then, set `sockets[network_array_position]` equal to that local variable we just made. That way, we can save the new socket to either the first or the second slot. Next, check whether `network_array_position` equals `0` (meaning that a client has connected to the first slot). If so, increment this variable since we should now be writing the next socket to the second slot in the `sockets` array.

After this, use the `show_message_async` function to notify the user that a client has connected. Finally, break the case.

Disconnection

Now, we'll handle the disconnection of a client. The constant for a disconnection is `network_type_disconnect`, so put in a case for that below the one for a connection. Then, inside, first check whether the socket that has disconnected (again held in the `"socket"` key, which is also available in connection and disconnection) equals the socket index held in `index 0` of our `sockets` array. If so, set that position to `-1`, and decrement our `network_array_position` variable. Otherwise, set the socket held in `index 1` of our `sockets` array to `-1`.

Next, verify that the socket held in `index 0` of our `sockets` array is not `-1`. Via this, we're going to tell the socket that is still there, if there is one, that the other player has disconnected. So we kind of lied before when we said what the buffer would be holding, by not mentioning `-2`. But we didn't mention it because the buffer will never be holding a `-2` alongside any of those other values. If the buffer has a `-2` in it for this purpose, it's not going to be holding any other values. So we didn't need to make the buffer larger than `2435` to accommodate a `-2`, since only the `-2` will be used and sent when there is a `-2`.

Whenever writing to a buffer, we must first seek its beginning, at least with fixed buffers. Seeking in a buffer is easy. Just use the `buffer_seek(buffer, base, offset)` function. Our buffer is `data_to_send_buff` of course. Our next parameter will be the constant `buffer_seek_start`, and the final one will be a `0`. When seeking, the function seeks `offset` number of positions from the `base`, so this function call right here will seek the exact start of the buffer.

Now, we can write a value to this buffer with the `buffer_write(buffer, type, value)` function. Our buffer is the same as the one we just seeked in, and the type shall be `buffer_f32` (unless, again, you're reading this when 16-bit floats can be used, in which case use `buffer_f16`). Finally, we will write a `-2`. So whenever a client disconnects, if there is another client still connected, we'll send a `-2` and the client that received this value will know that they are the only connected client.

The final thing we have to do is to send the buffer with the `network_send_packet(socket, buffer, size)` function. Since in this `if` statement, we checked whether the first socket slot was connected, we'll use that same socket here. Next, you should know what our buffer is. As for the size, before we had used the `buffer_get_size` function. However, this returns the size of all the data in your buffer. Keep in mind that we are not erasing the buffer every time we write to it, there's still the old data. So, if we used that function, it would send the old data, which we don't want. So to solve this, we'll use the `buffer_tell(buffer)` function, which tells you how many bytes in your "cursor", so to speak, is in the buffer. That way, we'll only send the value(s) that we just wrote. Make sure you don't seek anywhere else in the buffer when you're doing this though, and that you write in order, not seeking to the end of where you'll write and then somewhere in the middle. So use this function as our argument for the `size` parameter, and then you've successfully sent a `-2` to the client.

Now, make an `else if` statement that checks whether index 1 of our `sockets` array is not equal to `-1`. Copy the code you just wrote (from seeking to sending) and put it in this `else if`, but instead of having it sent to `sockets[0]`, have it sent to `sockets[1]`. So whenever a client disconnects, we'll tell the other client that is still connected (if there is one) that they are the only client connected.

Outside that `else if`, notify the user that a client has disconnected (again with an **Asynchronous** event of course, it's imperative that one be used; otherwise, the server will stop until the user interacts with the dialog). Then, you can break the case.

Handling data

Nice job, you've made it this far! We only have one more case to add, which is for when the server receives data. The constant for this is `network_type_data`, so add one final case for this.

Whenever we get data in a **Asynchronous Networking** event, we'll have two additional keys available to use: `"buffer"` and `"size"`. The first is the index of the buffer, and the second is its size. We don't care about the size for this game, but it's good for you to know about. The buffer index is destroyed after this event is over, so you have to handle it in this one, or save it.

Inside the case, check whether the value for the key `"id"` is equal to the first socket we have saved and verify that the second socket we have saved isn't -1 (as when we get data, we're going to send data to the other client, but it's redundant to send a nonexistent client). This `"id"` key is like the `"socket"` key, but it's for an existing connection, not a new or destroyed one. Usually, it holds the socket that triggered this event, but if the event was triggered in the server and the event was triggered for data, then this will hold the socket index of the client that sent the data. Anyway, inside of this `if` statement, call a script (that we'll soon make) called `scr_handle_data`, and pass it the buffer we received (using the DS Map key, we told you about in the previous paragraph) and 1. The script we will be creating will take two parameters: a buffer index and the one which the client needs to spit the data back out to. This second parameter of course uses zero-based indexing.

Otherwise, if the value for the key `"id"` equals the second socket we have saved and the first socket we have saved isn't -1 (we got data from the second socket and the first socket exists), set `index 1` of our `buffers` array to the buffer we received, and call the same script, passing it the same first parameter but 0 for the second parameter. Finally, (outside the `else` of course!), break the case.

The neat thing about the **Asynchronous Networking** event is that it can be triggered *whenever* there's a connection, disconnection, or a buffer received. As such, it can be triggered multiple times a step for two different buffers, so we don't have to worry about the data of only one client being handled.

Congratulations! You've sort of finished this networking event! Sort of, because you've still got a script to work on. Let's get working on that!

Our data handling script

So make a new script, and make sure to call it `scr_handle_data` so that the **Asynchronous Networking** event doesn't call a nonexistent script. Set the local variables `buff` to `argument0`, and `client_to_send_to` to `argument1`.

First, seek the beginning of the buffer we were passed. Next, we will read the first value of the buffer into the local variable `player_x` with the function `buffer_read(buffer, type)`. We'll be reading from the buffer we were passed; use the type of `buffer_f32` like before (unless, of course, you've been using 16-bit floats if it's supported). Now, do the same for the following local variables: `player_y`, `player_sprite`, `player_subimage`, and finally, `player_xscale`.

Once you've read in all the values, we'll send them back out to the other client. So first, seek the beginning of our `data_to_send_buff` buffer. Then, write the values to the buffer in the order you got them (first in, first out, unlike a stack in Assembly).

Finally, send this buffer to the socket in `sockets[client_to_send_to]`, and remember that we got that index as a parameter already. Also, use our `buffer_tell` method again to know the size of our buffer. When you're done with that, you're done with the script, so you can close the code editor there.

Nice job getting this far, but there's just one last thing we have to do. If the server closes before the clients do and there are two clients connected, we need to tell them both that the server has been shut down so that they don't continue to display the second player on screen. Clients don't have a disconnection event, so we can't test for that, instead we must have the server tell the clients directly that it has disconnected. This is really easy though. We're going to use basically the same method we used for when a client has disconnected.

So create a **Game End** event inside of your server. Inside, verify that *both* sockets are not equal to `-1` (meaning, we have two clients connected). Next, seek the beginning of our `data_to_send_buff` buffer. Write a `-2` to it. Then, we have a special way we're going to send this data to the clients—with a `for` loop. With networking, sending data can sometimes fail, and if we fail to send this data, then the client might think there's still a second player and display them even though they're not connected. So we're going to try multiple times with each send to give us the best chance of the `-2` being sent.

In the `for` loop, have a counter variable that starts with a value of `0` increment with each run of the loop. This loop should run as long as the function call that sends data to the client returns a value less than `0` (meaning it failed) and the counter variable is less than `5` (so we'll make a total of five attempts). You should have two of these, one for each different client.

Finally, destroy our server and delete our buffer.

This is the best we can get, aside from calling a `sleep` function in between sending the data and destroying the server or having a UDP stream that gets sent to the client. Doing this, however, would complicate this tutorial; we just want to teach you some basics. GameMaker used to have a sleep function, but they removed it. Alarms typically work as replacements, but the **Game End** event runs at the closing of your game/application, so you can't do anything after it (which, in this case, *would* be to use an alarm to wait before removing the server and buffer).

Great job! You've completed your server program. You can now move onto making your client system! Applaud yourself. Unfortunately, you can't test your server yet, as your client isn't yet created, but once it's been made, you can test your system.

The client in your client/server system

So you just finished half of the multiplayer system—the server. The other half that you have to create is your client, and that will go in the same project you were using in the rest of the game (where you put in views, and so on).

So open up your main project if it isn't open already. Inside, make a client object. First we will use the function get_string_async(string, default) to prompt the player for a server and port. The first parameter is the string you want displayed (the prompt itself), and the second is the textbox's default string. Prompt the player for the IP address and port number of the server they want to connect to, and have them type it in the format of IP:port (for example, our string parameter was "Type in the IP Address and the port of the server you wish to connect to in the format of IP:port. The IP and port are printed on the screen of the server."). Provide an empty string as the default string. You needn't save the index of the function call in a variable, since all of the times that we use a function that triggers an **Asynchronous Dialog** event will be for this same purpose.

After this, set the variable player_two to -1. It will later hold the index of the second player, if one is to connect. Then, set the variables server_ip and server_port both to an empty string (""). Next, set connected to false, as we have not yet connected to the server. After this, create a TCP socket with the function network_create_socket(type) and save the index to a variable called socket. And since we want a TCP socket, pass in network_socket_tcp. Finally, create a fixed buffer called buff with a size of 2435 (the same size as the one in the client), and align it to 4 bytes (or a 2 if you've been using 16-bit for the other parts of this chapter).

After that, you're done with your **Create** event. Now let's move onto the **Asynchronous Dialog** event. In here is where we will parse the string that the user input, separating it into an IP and port, and then we will attempt to connect to the provided server. If this fails at any point, we'll prompt the user for another string, telling them where they might've gone wrong. So first add in an **Asynchronous Dialog** event. Inside, set the local variable server_string equal to the "result" key of our async_load DS Map. Then, set server_ip and server_port to empty strings again, as this event could be run over and over again, and we need to reset those strings every time. Finally, set the local variable met_colon to false. A colon signifies the end of the IP address or URL and the beginning of a port number.

Once you've set up these variables, test whether server_string equals an empty string. This happens whenever the user hits the **Cancel** button or actually supplies nothing and hits the **Okay** button. If so, prompt the user again, telling them that they didn't supply an IP address or port number, and remind them of the format to type these in. If you want to put in a newline, use the # character. And don't provide a default string, as with the rest of the calls you'll make to this function in this event.

After this, put an `else` statement. The rest of the code for this event will go in there. At the top, put in a `for` loop. Set the local variable `i` to `1`. Have this loop run as long as it is less than `string_length(string) + 1`, where you pass the function the string `server_string`. Increment `i` after each iteration of the loop. The reason we didn't set the variable to `0` first and have the loop run while the variable is less than the length of the string, but rather we set it to `1` and had the loop run while it's less than the length plus 1 is because of the way strings are indexed. Strings are indexed from 1, not 0, so in the string `"Hello"`, the `"H"` is at index `1`, and the length is `5`. If we wanted to print this entire string out, character by character, we'd have to set a counter variable equal to `1` and then have the loop run while the counter is less than `6` (length plus one). If strings were indexed from `0`, we would run the loop as long as the counter was less than `5`, as lengths are always the literal and exact length.

Inside this loop, first set the local variable `substr` equal to `string_char_at(str, index)`. Our string to pass it will be `server_string`, and our index will be the value of our counter variable, `i`. This will set `substr` equal to the current character that we are looking at in the string that the user gave us.

Below this, put in another `for` loop (still nested in our previous one). Set another local counter variable called `a` equal to `48`, have the loop run as long as the counter is less than `58` and `met_colon` is `true`, and increment `a` in each iteration of the loop. In the ASCII table, the number 48 represents the character 0, and the number 58 represents the colon character. The number 57 represents the character 9 (the last digit), so the colon character directly follows the character 9. This loops runs as long as our counter represents the digits. Ports must always be numbers, and this loop we have here is going to prevent attempting to connect to a port number that isn't composed of just digits, which would throw us an error. The loop is only for the port, that is why we have it only run if `met_colon` is `true`. Inside this loop, test whether `substr = chr(val)`, where you pass the function `a`. If so, break out of the `for` loop with the `break` statement. Below this, put an `else if` that checks whether our counter equals `57` (so we're on the last possible legitimate character for a port, and our substring isn't that character). If so, prompt the user for a server and port again, and tell them they provided an invalid port. Again, remind them of the format. So, the loop will exit once the current character we'll be looking at is a digit, and if it's not, the user will be asked to provide a valid port.

Outside this loop, verify that our current character is not the colon (the IP versus port delimiter), and if we haven't met the colon yet. If so, add the current character to `server_ip`, like in the following code. We're showing you the code directly, since combining strings in GameMaker can get weird with what you can and can't do and how you do it. Sometimes, using a function will work, sometimes it won't work. At least in this case, it worked when we did it the following way:

```
server_ip = server_ip + substr;
```

So as long as we're not supposed to be writing to our port string, add the current character to the IP string. Below this, put an `else if` that checks whether the current character is the colon. If so, set `met_colon` to `true`.

Finally, put an `else` statement that adjoins the current character to the string `server_port` in the same way that we did it with the IP, as once we've met our delimiter character, we should be writing to the port string, not the IP string.

After that (and now your code will be outside the main `for` loop), put in an `if` statement. Have it check whether the port string is equal to an empty string (so no port number was parsed in). If so, add one more prompt for an IP and port and tell them that they didn't enter any port number, and remind them of the format to type the string in.

Below this should be an `else if` statement. Here, you will be attempting to connect (inside of the `else if` condition) to the server with the `network_connect(socket, url, port)`. The first parameter is the socket to connect with, which you made in the **Create** event of this object and called `socket`. The next parameter doesn't have to be a URL, it can be an IP address as well, which we'll be using here. The third parameter is the port. So pass in the socket you made before in this object, `server_ip`, and `real(server_port)`, as the third parameter is supposed to be a number, not a string. The `real` function returns its string argument as a number. Then, check whether the connection function returned a value less than `0` (the connection failed). If so, tell the user that the client failed to connect to the provided server because either the wrong IP and port were provided, or the connection actually failed. Also, tell them the format to type in their response to the prompt.

After this, add a final `else` statement, wherein you set `connected` to `true`, as the connection to the server was successful and you can now send and receive data with it.

Now let's add our **Step** event where we send data to the server. Inside, test whether we're connected to the server (so `connected` will be `true`). Inside, we're going to be sending data about the player to the server. So we have to start with seeking the start of the buffer, which if you remember, we called `buff`. Next, write the x and y coordinates of the player and make sure to use the same type you've been using all along. Then, check whether the player's `sprite_index` is the walking sprite. If so, write a `0` to the buffer. Otherwise (since you should only have two sprites for the player in this game), write a `1`. After this, write the player's `image_index`, and then their `image_xscale`. Finally, send the buffer over the socket that the client object created.

Once you've finished that, we have to put in code for when the client receives data. Add a **Asynchronous Networking** event. Check whether the event type was `network_type_data` (so check the `"type"` key in `async_load`). Next, load the buffer we received into a local variable called `received_buff`. Then, seek its beginning. Read its first value into a local variable called `buffer_first_val`. We're reading it into this first because the first value is either going to be `-2` or the x coordinate of the player in the other client. Check whether this new variable equals `-2` and if an instance of the other player exists (using the `instance_exists(object)` function, where you pass it what you will be naming the other object). If so, use the `with` statement (passing it `player_two`) to destroy the instance of the other player.

Next, put in an `else if` clause that checks whether `buffer_first_val` is not equal to `-2` (so we know why the above `if` statement wasn't triggered and are running the proper code), where the rest of the code for this event will go. Assign `player_x` (which must not be local, nor can any of the other variables made in the event after now be) to be equal to `buffer_first_val`. Then, read in the y coordinate. After this, test whether the value you read in is a `0`. If so, `player_two_sprite` should equal what you will name the walking sprite. Otherwise, it should equal what you will name the jumping sprite. Then, read in a value to `player_two_subimage` and `player_two_xscale`.

After this, verify that an instance doesn't exist of the other player object (making sure to use the same name you used before). If one doesn't exist, assign `player_two` to equal the return value of `instance_create`, when you create the other player at (`player_x`, `player_y`) so that the variable will hold the index of this other player object.

Then, use a `with` statement, passing it the index of the other player object. Assign x to `other.player_x`. `other.player_x` will be referencing `player_x` in the client, since you're in a `with` statement right now, and x will reference the x coordinate of the instance you passed to the `with` statement. Do the same for the other variables (y, `sprite_index`, `image_index`, and finally `image_xscale`).

Great job! You're almost done with the client. We have only a few more things to do. Add a **Game End** event to the client object. Inside, delete the buffer called `buff`, and then delete our socket. Now you can put the client into your room.

The final part is to actually create the second player object and its sprites. As far as the sprites, you can actually import existing sprite files if you right-click on the **Sprites** folder in the resource tree, and select **Add Existing Sprite**. Navigate to `<Project root directory>\sprites` and import the proper `.gmx` files (although you have to do them one at a time) that you see there. By importing the sprite, you'll essentially be making a complete copy, but GameMaker will automatically attach `_new` to the end of the name of the copy. What you'll want to change in the copies is the color scheme, as well as what they're called. Make sure that their names are the same as the ones you used in the **Asynchronous Networking** event for the client object so that nothing fails. Then, create a second player object (and again, make sure to use the same name as in the client object) and assign it the walking sprite in the object's main properties editor screen. You don't need to do anything else to the object.

Now, the unfortunate thing about this networking section is that you couldn't really test small amounts of code bit by bit as much as you would have liked, so it'll be a bit harder to find issues in your code. However, it's not horribly impossible, as you should be able to see the general area of where your issues took place. Start with just testing your game with one client and one server to see if you can connect and so on. Then, once all that works, use the keyboard shortcut *Ctrl + Alt + C* when in your client project. Make sure to choose **Single runtime executable (*.exe)** under the **Save as type** section of the dialog that opens. That way you can easily have two instances of the client open on a single computer. Once the client executables have been made, run the server from the regular compile in GameMaker (you don't have to make an executable), and then run two instances of your client on the same computer. Connect both to the server, and move around in both. You should see that the second player object in each client moves around. If it does, great job! If it's not working, you might want to check your firewall settings to see if that could be blocking a connection; sometimes, it does this by default for local connections. Otherwise, check your code for any errors. In the end of all this, our setup will look like the following:

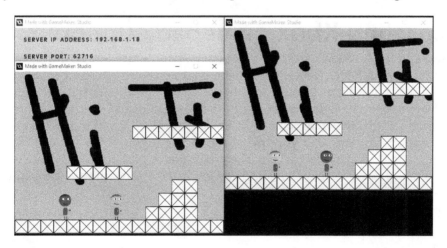

If you can, get three computers, put one client on one, another client on another, and a server on the third. That should work too! If you can't get three, but you can get two, do the same thing, but, of course, on two computers. And if you can, try setting up a web host, running the server there, and connecting to the URL, not the IP address of the web host. That should work too, since the function we used for connecting to a server accepts URLs; or if you don't have a web host, but you do have some kind of external IP address that people can connect to (if you're going to have to change your router's settings, like when setting up a web server, we advise you not to try this and be satisfied with the other tests), try running the server on this external IP and connecting to the external IP address rather than a local one.

Yay! You're done with the networking section of your game! Applaud yourself. Seriously. Networking is a much more difficult section, and it's got kinks to work out, since it's one of the things that can be more prone to errors, even if you think all your code is good. But you made it! If there was anything you were confused about, reread those bits. You don't need to know them for the next section, but you should review those parts while they're fresh in your head.

A final note though about networking. Often, you'll want to see what was sent from what machine to what other machine so that you can trace issues, and for that there is the program Wireshark (`https://www.wireshark.org`). The only unfortunate thing about it is that it cannot read data that is sent from one machine to itself (so for instance if you have your client and server all running on a single computer, it can't see that data) because it gets data sent from Ethernet drivers, and, at least, on Windows, data that doesn't need to leave the machine will not reach there. So, when using Wireshark, make sure to have, at least, two computers.

But anyway, once you're ready, move onto putting Xbox gamepad support into your game.

Integrating Xbox gamepad support

This next and final section will show you how to incorporate Xbox controls into your game. Remember however, this section is completely optional if you do not have an Xbox controller on hand to test. In such a case, external programs exist that allow the player to bind a button press, joystick direction, and so on, on a controller to a keypress so that they still can use an Xbox controller, even if it isn't completely official support. You can refer your players to these programs. Two that we have heard of are **JoyToKey** and **Xpadder**. Their websites are at `http://joytokey.net/en` and `http://www.xpadder.com`. Both are great and allow multiple game profiles.

If you do however have an Xbox controller on hand and would like to learn how to incorporate support for it into your games, continue on.

GameMaker has two different kinds of gamepad support. One of them is legacy, not yet obsolete and still available for use, but not recommended and also only for Windows, and the other is the updated version with more functionality. The legacy support most likely relies on the old DInput system, whereas the modern one most likely XInput, but there could be other things at play when it comes to the difference between legacy and modern gamepad support in GameMaker.

While it would seem obvious to jump into the updated one, we found that one of our relatively new Xbox controllers actually needed the legacy support and could not function with the more current support. On that note though, most players probably use devices that would use the new functionality, but it would not be bad to include support for the other form of gamepad support, especially since it's really easy. So it's probably best to include both.

To test which functionality will work for your device, we can use a debug message. At the top of the **Step** event for your player object (since GameMaker might not immediately recognize the gamepad being plugged in, so it's not good to put this in the **Create** event, at least for this small game, and we want the player to be able to plug in a gamepad at any time), put the following code. If `joystick_exists(id)`, where id can be 1 or 2 for two total slots, pass it 1 for the first slot, returns `true`, then show a message that says so. Then, below that check whether `gamepad_is_connected(slot)`, where slot can be from 0 to however many controllers the device the game is running on supports, returns `true` when you pass it 0 for slot. If so, show a message different from the first. The first function is for the legacy support, the second is for the newer gamepad support. Run the game to see which version your gamepad supports.

Either way, it's probably in your best interest to put in code for both, even if your gamepad won't support both, but you should know at which phase of this section your gamepad will definitely work. So let's start with the actual gamepad support.

Legacy gamepad support

We'll start with the older version's code. In your `if` statement where you checked if a joystick exists (you just put it in), instead of having it display a debug message, have it set the local variable `joystick_connected` to `true`. Otherwise, set it to `false` so that we are always checking if the gamepad is plugged in. In both assignments, you'll have to make the variable local so that it's always properly created.

Then, find where you checked for a keypress of the spacebar. Add an OR operator and put in a set of parentheses, so that the total Boolean value of what we're about to put in will be checked with that OR. Inside this set of parentheses, check whether we have a joystick connected and whether the *A* button is pressed. To check for a button press, use the function `joystick_check_button(id, numb)`. The id parameter is the same as before, but numb is the numerical value of the button you want to check for. The following is a chart for the numerical values. The numb parameter can be up to 32, but the Xbox controller doesn't have 32 buttons:

A	B	X	Y	Left button	Right button	Back button	Start button	Left joy press	Right joy press
1	2	3	4	5	6	7	8	9	10

Nice job, you've got on board with the working of the legacy system. We'll now program left and right movement. Highlight all of the code between incrementing vspd if it's less than 15 and testing whether both or neither of the left and right arrow keys are being pressed, and deleted. We're going to start afresh. In the spot where all that code was, first declare a local variable called using_controller, and set it to false. After this, put in an if statement that checks whether our joystick is connected and if the stick itself returns a value less than or equal to -0.1 or greater than or equal to 0.1. To check the value of a joystick using legacy support, use the function `joystick_xpos(id)`. Legacy support doesn't have a built in dead-zone, so we must see if the value we get is outside that range of 10 percent. In the end, your if statement's condition will look like the following:

```
if (joystick_connected && ((joystick_xpos(1) >= 0.1) ||
(joystick_xpos(1) <= -0.1))) { <...> }
```

Inside of here, set our horizontal speed (remember to use our own variable called hspd) equal to five times of whatever value we got the joystick. In this way, the player can vary their speed. Then, set using_controller to true, since we are using the controller of course!

Outside this, put an else clause. Inside of it should be two different if statements. The first should check whether we're pressing the right key, and if so our horizontal speed should be 5. The next should test if we're pressing the left key, and if so, our horizontal speed should be set to -5.

Finally, put your cursor on the line with the `if` statement that checks whether both of the arrow keys are being pressed. Add two OR operators and two sets of parentheses after each. Inside the first set, check whether the right key is being held and if the controller's joystick is being used. In the second set, do the same, but for the right key. In the end, the `if` statement will run in the following conditions:

*   Both arrow keys are being pressed
*   Both arrow keys are being pressed and the joystick is being pushed
*   One key is being pressed and the joystick is being pushed

Nice, there's nothing else to do for legacy support. If your controller required it from the test before, you can run your game. Otherwise, just move onto the newer support section.

Modern gamepad support

Now, we'll do the current support. At the top of the **Step** event for the player, where you checked if the gamepad is connected and showed a debug message if so, have it set `gamepad_connected` to `true` instead of showing a message. Otherwise, set it to `false`.

Great. Now we can do the jumping. After the code where you check if the **A** button has been pressed using legacy code, add another OR operator and another set of parentheses. Check whether our gamepad is connected, and if the **A** button has been pressed. Button presses are a lot easier on the gamepad. You use the function `gamepad_button_check(slot, button)`, where the slot is the same as before, and as for the button, there is a list of constants in the documentation under **Reference | Mouse, Keyboard, and Other Controls | Gamepad Input**. Find the constant for the **A** button and then call this function.

Nice job! You're done with the jumping for the modern gamepad support, now we must put in the left and right movement. This is actually very easy. In between the `if` statement that checks if the legacy gamepad is connected and if its joystick is outside of a specific dead-zone, and the `else` clause below it, and an `else if` statement. Inside, check if the gamepad is connected. Inside the `else if` statement, set our horizontal speed equal to five times the value of the left joystick's x axis. To find this value, use the function `gamepad_axis_value(slot, axisIndex)`. For the second parameter, find the constant on the documentation page we just supplied you that represents the left joystick's x axis. After you've set our horizontal speed, verify that it is not equal to 0. If so, set `using_controller` to `true`. Modern gamepad support has a built-in dead-zone system, wherein if the joystick returns value within the dead-zone, the function just returns a 0, so our horizontal speed won't be anything other than 0 unless the player bumps their joystick enough.

Great job! You're done with the newer gamepad support. Even if your joystick was only going to support legacy code anyway, it's still good to play your game again to ensure you didn't mess up the newer support's code and in turn mess up the legacy code. So either way, test your game to ensure once and for all that your gamepad support works.

If it does, congratulations! We just have one last note about gamepads. It is, unfortunately, significantly harder to put in a rebinding system, as there's no equivalent of the variable `keyboard_lastkey` for gamepads. You will need to check whether the button press was this button, or this button, and so on. It's not undoable, you can use a `switch` statement in fact; but you should know that you won't be able to get the same efficiency we had in *Chapter 4, Fun with Infinity and Gravity – An Endless Platformer* without the use of external DLLs and a GameMaker extension.

But anyway, nice job! You're done with the chapter, and it's time to move onto the summary.

Summary

Congrats! You've finished this chapter. That was one hefty chapter, huh? But you finished it, so great job. As usual, you should go review the chapter and refresh your brain on some of the things you learned. Once you've done that, move on to the *Review questions*, followed by the *Quick drills*.

Review questions

1. What is `image_xscale`, and what was the problem we would've had with it had we not centered the origin of the player sprite?
2. How do you import a spritesheet?
3. What are views, and what is the port on screen?
4. Describe all of the networking terms we explained to you earlier: buffer, packet, TCP, UDP, socket, port, client/server networking, and IP address.
5. What is byte alignment?
6. What must you do before reading and writing to a fixed buffer?
7. What were the two different kinds of gamepad support we incorporated, and what are some of the differences between them?

Quick drills

1. Allow the player to press a key to join a server (rather than having the popup appear immediately). If they want to join a server, make sure they aren't currently connected to one. If they are, then disconnect them from that server before joining them to the new one.

2. Now, allow pressing a button on an Xbox controller to do the same thing. Make sure to incorporate both legacy and modern gamepad support.

Great job! You've completed this entire chapter. Applaud yourself one last time, and again review anything you were confused about. In the next chapter, we'll create a scrolling shooter game, such as Namco's *Xevious*. Let's get going!

7
Programming a Scrolling Shooter

In this chapter, we will provide an overview of the creation of a scrolling shooter game (such as the classic *Xevious* by Namco or *Guxt* by Studio Pixel). By design, a scrolling shooter typically has a scrolling background and the player tries to avoid obstacles and enemies while shooting down the enemies. The game can be one infinite level or broken into different levels depending on the design implemented. Think about some scrolling shooters you might have played against, and if you haven't played any, try *Guxt* (`http://cavestory.org/pixels-works/guxt.php`). It's great! This chapter will cover object parenting, AI, a new kind of event, the paths resource, and particles. It's time to get started!

Creating the main ship

The first step in our game will be to create our main ship, controlled by the player. Make a new GameMaker project. We're going to make this game in a little retro style, so draw two subimages for your main ship's sprite, one for forward, and one for tilting right (which we will repurpose for tilting left with `image_xscale`). Typically in games of this style, no extra sprite will exist for moving downward, and it will use the same one as for moving forward. The subimages should be 32 x 32, to make some things easier later on. When creating your ship, give it two guns, one on each side. An example is shown as follows:

Once you have made your ship's subimages, modify the sprite's bounding box as usual, and also make sure to center the origin (on both axes) so that we don't run into any issues with image_xscale and so that we can easily program the vertical movement, accounting for going off of the screen. After this, create the object for your main ship and assign it the ship sprite.

In the **Create** event of your new ship object, set our subimage's cycling speed to 0 (image_speed=0;) so that we don't loop through the images. After this, add a **Step** event, where we will program the movement and animation. We will reuse some of the code from the previous chapter for this part since that code worked really well. As you develop more games, you will want to utilize resources from other games wherever you can rather than recreating everything from scratch:

1. First, set the local variables hspd and vspd to 0, as we did in the previous chapter. Make sure to always use these variables when we talk about horizontal or vertical speed.

2. Next, check if we have pressed the up key. If so, set our vertical speed to -6. Then, check whether we've pressed the down key, and if so, set our vertical speed to positive 6. Then check whether we've pressed both of the left and right arrow keys. If so, our vertical speed should be 0. Put in the same code, but for the left and right arrow keys, and for our horizontal speed, of course.

3. Once you've done that, we'll program the animation. First, check whether we're moving left or right at all. If so, set our subimage to the one of the ship moving forward. Otherwise, if our horizontal speed is greater than 0 (meaning that we are moving to the right), correctly assign our current subimage to that of moving right, and also accordingly set image_xscale. Finally, put an else that does the same thing, except the difference will be that image_xscale should be the opposite of what you previously defined it as.

There's just one more thing to program in the **Step** event, making the ship actually move. First, put in an if statement that checks whether by moving from our current y position by vspd pixels would have our y coordinate be greater than or equal to the height of our room (remember the room_height variable from *Chapter 4, Fun with Infinity and Gravity – An Endless Platformer*?) or have it be less than or equal to 0. Use place_meeting for the collision checking.

Inside the if statement, put a while loop that runs as long as moving by y + sign(vspd) pixels (as in the previous chapter) wouldn't have the y coordinate of the ship object be equal to the height of our room or 0. Inside the loop, increment y by sign(vpsd). Then, outside of this loop, set our vertical speed to 0. Outside the if statement, increment y by our vertical speed. This code is basically the exact same as what we used in the previous chapter, so it shouldn't be confusing. Basically, if moving by 1 pixel would have the middle of the ship (since we completely centered the origin), go past the top or bottom of the room, we'll move until that happens.

Copy all the code and paste it below, but replace all uses of y with x, all uses of vspd with hspd, and all uses of room_height with room_width.

When you're done with that, create a room, put your ship object in it, and test your game. Make sure that the ship can fly all around, but that at least half of it will always appear onscreen (or a quarter in the case of going into the corners of the room). If all that works, you can move onto the creation of our enemies.

Creating the enemies

The next step in our game will be to program the enemies and give them a simple AI. The first part of the process is to create an enemy sprite. Since we're going to have you create an enemy with a specific routine, you should either use the sprite provided in the example project or you should create a 32 x 32 enemy sprite with a single subimage that is intended to rotate and shoot two bullets, one out of each side. When you're done with creating the subimage, modify the mask as usual and also center the origin of the sprite. After this, create an enemy object and assign it the proper sprite.

Parenting in objects

GameMaker uses the object-oriented programming paradigm, as you've probably noticed by now. Most of what we do is in objects, and even the resources that aren't called objects are actually objects in terms of object-oriented programming. They just can't do what GameMaker objects do. So rooms are objects, backgrounds are objects, *everything* is an object. And what is an object really? It's an area of memory with a bunch of data in it. GameMaker has different kinds of objects. We will focus on objects as defined by GameMaker, as these are the objects where most of our programming exists. The other types of objects don't share all the same variables. For example, your backgrounds can't really use the x variable. But they can use the hspeed variable. The regular objects and everything else are distinct from one another, even though they're all technically objects.

Now that we have a better understanding of objects (just an area of memory that holds data), we can think about what this can mean. If an object is just an area of memory that holds a bunch of data, and the object itself is data, can we have objects within objects?

Yes! If you already have experience with object-oriented programming, you probably already know this, but for those of you who don't, having objects within objects is where you have parent objects and child objects. Child objects are contained in parent objects, and they inherit properties from their parent object. You can even have a child object also be a parent object!

Parenting can also group objects, so instead of checking for a collision for every individual enemy, we can just check for a collision with a parent, and assign this parent object children. This is what we will be doing in this game.

Now you might be wondering, "How do I use this powerful tool?" Don't worry, we'll show you right now. First make an object called `class_enemy` (as we're basically going to create an `enemy` class as if we were using another language such as C++ or Java). Give it a **Step** event wherein you check whether its x or y coordinates are outside the room, or whether the variable `hp` (set by children of this object) is less than 1. Destroy the instance, if so.

Now, we can give the object child objects. Open up the regular enemy object so that you can choose its parent (done via the main properties page for any object), as shown in the following screenshot:

To assign a parent, just click on the little menu icon next to the **Parent** box to open a contextual menu (that's what they're called if you didn't know) that lists all the objects you can choose from. Choose the object we created, called `class_enemy`. Once you've assigned this object as a parent, you can open up the parent object and you should see `obj_enemy` (assuming that's what you called it) as a child in the **Children** box.

Now that you've set this up, we can actually work on the enemy itself. Before we do that, let's make a bullet. Make a small bullet sprite, one that will look good with your enemy's sprite. Of course, modify the mask and center the origin.

Then, make a bullet object, make it a child of `class_enemy`. Give it a **Create** event, wherein you set the variable `hp` to 5. We're going to give all children of `class_enemy` a health system so that they can all be destroyed by the player's bullets. Next, add a **Step** event. Inside, call the function `event_inherited()`. By default, when a parent object and a child object both share an event (say, for example, they both have a **Step** event, as we have), the child will not run the parent's event. But by calling the function, it will, so that the child will run both events.

Next, we're going to use a function we haven't used in a while, `collision_rectangle(x, y, x2, y2, obj, prec, notme)`. Recall that it returns either `noone` or the index of the object you were looking for that happened to be in that range. Check for a collision with the main ship object within the same range as the bounding box you gave the enemy's bullet's sprite. Destroy the bullet if the function's return value is not equal to `noone`.

Now that you're done with the bullet, we can go back to the enemy. Inside the enemy's **Create** event, set the variable `can_shoot` to `true`. Add an event for **Alarm 0**, wherein you allow the enemy to shoot again.

Now we can get to work on the enemy's **Step** event. First, check whether its `hp` is less than `1` (as objects should always check whether they should be destroyed before they do anything). Destroy the instance if so.

Below this, we will make the `enemy` object spin. This is done by using the `image_angle` variable, which ranges from `0` to `359` and uses the same system as the `direction` variable (with 0 being right, 90 being up, and so on). Check whether the variable is less than `358`. If so, increment it by 2. Otherwise, set it to `0` (which 359 is one degree less than, as 0 is equivalent to 359, but we are of course using 2 for our increase, as with a room speed of 30, incrementing by 1 is slow).

After this, we can give the enemy a tracking AI, wherein it will follow the player until it hits a certain range, then it'll just shoot. Add an `if` statement to check whether an instance of the main ship exists (otherwise, we can get an error by accidentally referencing an object that isn't in the room) using the `instance_exists(obj)` function from the previous chapter. Most of the code for this **Step** event will be included here.

The next function we'll use is `distance_to_object(obj)`, and we're sure you can guess its parameter and return value. Have the `if` statement run if the enemy's distance from the player is less than or equal to `200`. If so, set our `speed` to `0` (since we should no longer be moving). Below this, but still inside the `if` statement, check whether `can_shoot` is `true`. If so, create two variables, `bullet_one` and `bullet_two`. *Do not* make them local, otherwise, we can't reference them in a `with` statement. Assign them to two different calls to `instance_create`, with which you make bullet objects in the center of the enemy.

Next, add two `with` statements, one for each variable. In the first, we will be setting the speed and direction of the bullet with the `motion_set(dir, speed)` function. The direction should be the `image_angle` of the `enemy` object (referenced in the `with` statement with `other.image_angle`). The speed should be `10`. After this, set the `image_angle` of the bullet to the `image_angle` of the enemy so that it all lines up correctly.

Everything you put in the preceding `with` statement can go into the second. We'll add a bit to it though. First off, the direction of this second bullet should be the opposite of the enemy's (and in turn, that of the other bullet). You can do this by adding `180` in the first parameter for `motion_set`. Secondly, the horizontal scaling should also be the opposite, so set the `image_xscale` of the second bullet to the opposite of the first bullet. Do this by setting it equal to `-1` times `other.bullet_one.image_xscale`.

After this (but still inside the `if` statement for `can_shoot`), set **Alarm 0** to 30 steps, and then set `can_shoot` to `false`. Based on the default room speed, 30 steps is equal to one second. So, in this case, we are slowing the shooting down to one shot per second. Once the timer is activated, the enemy will be able to shoot again.

Now we've just got a little more code to write. After the `if` statement where you check if the enemy is within range of the main ship, add an `else` clause. Inside, first declare a local variable called `dir` that will hold the direction that the main ship is in, in relation to the enemy ship. For this, use the `point_direction(x, y, x2, y2)` function, where you pass it the enemy's coordinate's and the player's coordinates.

Then, paste in the following `if` statement. Generally, we don't just paste the raw code in without having you attempt it first, as that's bad practice, but this is a rather complex `if` statement, so we will provide you with the code and explain it so you can understand what is happening:

```
if ((dir >= 315 || dir <= 45) && !collision_rectangle(x + 16,
y - 16, x + 26, y + 16, class_enemy, false, true))
 || (dir > 45 && dir <= 135 && !collision_rectangle(x - 16,
y - 26, x + 16, y - 16, class_enemy, false, true))
 || (dir > 135 && dir <= 225 && !collision_rectangle(x - 26,
y - 16, x - 16, y + 16, class_enemy, false, true))
 || (dir > 225 && dir < 315 && !collision_rectangle(x - 16,

y + 16, x + 16, y + 26, class_enemy, false, true))
```

Let's break down this `if` statement. What it does is, it tests whether there is another enemy in the area we'll be moving through. Let's begin with the first part. First, we must test in its own set of parentheses if our direction is greater than or equal to `315` or (`||`) less than or equal to `45`. The `||` (OR) operator indicates that either of these statements must be true in order to execute the code. This region is a quarter circle that corresponds to the right direction in GameMaker. It's a diagonal quarter though (so not perfectly up and down lines, if you were to draw the quarter on the "circle").

Then, we check if there is also no other enemy on the right side. The `&&` (AND) operator indicates that both of these statements must be true. The first coordinate we passed to the function is the complete right edge of the object's sprite, up at its top. The second is 10 pixels away from the edge (on the *x* axis), and all the way at the bottom. For the last parameter (which is `notme`, if you recall), it is imperative that we pass `true`, otherwise it's possible that the instance of the enemy calling the function could make the function return true. That entire section is contained in its own set of parentheses of course, to separate it from the others.

The other sections are basically the same. However, for testing direction, we use `&&` (AND) and not `||` (OR), as for the first section, no number can be `315` or more, and still be less than or equal to `45`, but for the other directions, the numbers are in a range where the numbers flow into one another. You'll also notice that the coordinates are different, as we are testing different regions. The rectangle checked is always 10 pixels long on the axis that corresponds to the direction we're checking. It might help if you draw the rectangles on a coordinate plane to try to map it all out.

Basically, each section is evaluated (it checks if the player is on the right and if that side is free of enemies, then if the player is in the north and if that side is free of enemies, and so on) and then we use an `OR` operator in between each of them because each section only returns true if the section corresponds to the current direction of the player, in relation to the enemy, so we will essentially be checking as follows: is it the right section and is that free, or is it the top section and is that free, or is it the left section and is that free, or is it the bottom section and is that free? It's a rather complex `if` statement, but once you break it down, it's not so confusing.

Now, we will set the speed and direction of the enemy with `motion_set` if the statement returns `true`. The direction is the player's direction in relation to us, which we stored in the local variable `dir`, and a speed of `3` was appropriate. After this, directly outside that big `if` statement that we just wrote, put in an `else` clause that sets the `speed` to `0`. Then, outside of the `if` statement that checks whether or not an instance of the main ship exists, put an `else` clause that also sets the enemy's speed to `0`.

Great job! You've finished programming the enemy. We've just got to add one line of code to the main ship. At the very end of its **Step** event, after you increment x by hspd, check if the main ship has collided with an instance of the `class_enemy` object (using the `place_meeting` function). If so, destroy the main ship.

Now open up your room editor. Add a few instances of the enemy object into your room, then run your game. Is everything working perfectly? If so, great job! But you probably noticed that our player is defenseless! Well that's not right, is it?

Let's incorporate a quick shooting system. Create a small bullet sprite, modify the collision box, and center the origin of course. Then create an object for the player's bullet, and give it a **Create** event. Set its speed to 10 and direction to 90 (up).

Add a **Step** event. Inside, declare a local variable called enemy_hit, and use collision_rectangle to get the index of any enemies the bullet hits. Check whether the variable is equal to noone. If not, decrement hp of the enemy by 5, with enemy_hit.hp -= 5. Then, destroy the bullet. After this, outside the if statement, check whether the bullet's y coordinate is less than 0 (as the bullet can only be shot up). Destroy the instance of the bullet if so.

Now that you've finished the bullet, we have to let the ship shoot it. In the **Create** event for the main ship, set can_shoot to true. Also, set it to true in the **Alarm 0** event for this object.

Then, at the end of the **Step** event for the main ship object, check whether the player has pressed the spacebar, and whether they can shoot. If so, set can_shoot to false and set **Alarm 0** to 15 steps. Then, create two instances of the player's bullet object on opposite sides of it. Try to get them to line up with wherever you placed the guns in the sprite. Once you're done with that, you're done with all the shooting! Test your game to make sure that you're able to shoot and destroy the enemy with two bullets.

Random enemy spawning

The next step in our game will be to randomly spawn the enemies for variation in the game.

For this, create an object called obj_control. In its **Create** event, set the variable alarm_num to 300. We'll be using this variable to decide for when the alarm in this object should be triggered. 300 steps with a room speed of 30 is 10 seconds.

Then, set the random seed for the game using the same method we've been using for a few chapters, which is shown as follows since we haven't used it in a while:

```
random_set_seed(date_get_second_of_year(date_current_datetime()));
```

Following this, perform the **Alarm 0** event with event_perform. Pass the function ev_alarm and 0. Inside the object's Alarm 0 event, put an if statement that checks whether the main ship exists. Inside the if statement, create a switch statement for generating a random integer from 0 to 2 (inclusive of course!). In each case, generate different patterns of enemies. You might want to use the room editor to get the right coordinates. Remember to break each case!

Outside the `if` statement, set **Alarm 0** to `alarm_num`. Then check whether `alarm_num` is greater than `120` (4 seconds). If so, decrement it by 5. In this way, the time between enemy spawns will always be at least 4 seconds.

When you're done with all that, close out the object. We'll add more to it later of course, but we needn't add anything more yet. Open up the room editor and delete the enemy objects you already had in there. Put an instance of `obj_control` in the top-left corner of the room. Play your game and make sure that the frequency of enemies increases, and that the patterns are random, but that the patterns appear only within 4 seconds or more of each other. If you're done with that, we'll move onto programming a boss for the player to fight.

Programming a Boss AI

In this section, we'll be programming in a Boss AI for the player to fight after a certain time (a minute specifically). Create a missile sprite where its head points downwards (to make launching it from the boss easier to code), and of course, center its origin. Then, create a boss object and a missile object. We'll work on the boss later, but we'll have to reference it in the missile object.

Make the missile object a child of `class_enemy`, give it a depth of `-10`, and of course assign it its sprite. In the **Create** event for the object, give it two variables: `hp`, which should be set to `5`, and `dir`, which should be set to `270`. `dir`. This will be the default direction of the missile to face.

Now, add a **Step** event to the object. First call `event_inherited()`. Next, check if an instance of the boss object collides with the bottom of the missile (using `place_meeting`). If so, increment `y` by `5`. What this does is have the missile move down out of the boss' launchers until it's outside and can move freely.

After that, add an `else` clause. Inside, check whether an instance of the main ship exists. If so, set `dir` to the direction of the main ship in relation to the missile. Then set `image_angle` to `dir + 90`. We need the `+ 90` because the missile sprite faces downward, by default, so if `dir` holds `270` (down), we need `image_angle` to equal `360` (equivalent to 0), as that would have the missile use the default angle for its sprite. After that, use `motion_set` to make the missile chase the player at a speed of `5`.

Now, we can work on the boss itself. Create a sprite for a boss that would appear at the top of the screen with two launchers on either side, or just use the one provided in the example project to make things simpler. Center the origin and change the collision mask as usual. Then, go back to that boss object you made earlier; make it a child of class_enemy, give it its sprite, and set its depth to -20. In the **Create** event of the object, set the variables hp to 200 and alarm_num to 120. Then, perform the **Alarm 0** event.

Inside that event, add an if statement that checks whether the main ship exists. If so, put in a switch statement wherein you generate a random integer from 0 to 1 (inclusive of course!). Create two cases for them. Inside each, either spawn two instances of the enemy object out of either launcher, or two instances of the missile object. Make sure to break the cases. Outside, set **Alarm 0** to alarm_num.

Next, add a **Step** event to the boss object. Inside, put an if statement that checks whether hp is less than 1. If so, create an instance of obj_destroy_enemies (and we will create this object right after this). Then destroy the boss. After this, check whether the top half of the boss is less than 0 (we're going to have this boss move down into the view, spawning outside of the room at first). Increment y if so.

Before we forget, let's create that object to destroy the rest of the enemies. Make that object, and in its **Create** event, set **Alarm 0** to 5 steps. Now, open up the **Step** event, and inside, check whether the number of instances of class_enemy is more than 1 (use instance_number(obj) for this). If so, put in a with statement that destroys the nearest instance of that object by using the function instance_nearest(x, y, obj). This will eventually destroy all the enemies. Add an else clause (so this will have run if there are no more enemies) wherein the object destroys itself. Then, set **Alarm 0** to 5 (outside the else clause).

Now we're going to implement a resource called **Paths**. This resource allows you to force an object to travel along a certain path without having to store positions in an array or something like that. Paths make everything very simple. The first thing we must do is to create a path, of course. Close your boss object, we'll return to it later. Create a new path called path_boss. The editor might look daunting, but not if you know what you need. First, in the grid, the green box is the start point of the path, the red point is the one you've selected, and blue ones are any other points. You also should know that you can display the background of a room in the editor so you know how to set up our points. Display the main room by selecting the gray box on the top bar that says **<Select Room Background>** and choosing it from the drop-down menu. Finally, set the grid snaps to 32 (the boxes are labeled as **Snap X** and **Snap Y**), which is the same as the room editor's snaps.

So now that your editor is set up, we can plot our points. First, move the green box point to the horizontal middle of the room background area, and make sure to move it down vertically from the top so that it is in the same position as the boss' y coordinate after it's moved fully onto the screen. Then, click anywhere to make another point. The next point should be on the right side of the original one, so that when the boss moves to it, its right edge will be nearly against the edge of the room. Add another point just like this, but on the left edge. Now you might be wondering what the **sp** box is for. This is the speed percentage. When you set this path, you also set a speed. If you were to set a speed of 4 when you begin the path, a speed percentage of 100 would have the object using the path move at a speed of 4. With a speed percentage of 75, it would move at a speed of 3. Keep the percentage at 100 for all three points. The **Closed** checkbox will make the last point the same as the start point—a closed loop.

When you're done with that, close the path editor, and open your boss object. We have one final event to add—a **User defined** event. These events are special in that they're not special to GameMaker. What that means is that you can give your objects events that GameMaker doesn't assign any special actions to, and that it doesn't always run. So while the **Create** event is run *whenever* an object is created, your **User defined** event is run whenever you want it to be run with the event_perform (or any similar) function. You have a total of 16 of these types of events available to you, which should be more than enough. So if you wanted to run a special event whenever something takes damage, you could do that with this! To create one of these events, select the **other** | **User defined** | **User 0** in the dialog for adding a new event. Inside, check whether alarm_num is more than 60 (two seconds). Decrement that variable by 5 if so that whenever the boss is hit, it will increase the frequency with which it launches missiles or enemies.

You've now finished the boss object, so you can close it. We have some quick code to add in the player bullet object that is specially tailored for hitting the boss. Open that object's **Step** event. Right after you decrement the hp variable of the enemy that has been hit, put in an if statement. Use the object_get_name(obj) function, which takes an instance of an object as input, and outputs the name you provided it in the project's resource tree. In our case, we'll pass it enemy_hit, and the return value we'll look for is the string "obj_boss".

Inside the if statement, check whether the boss' hp is equal to 100. If so, we'll make it start a path. You can do this by calling the path_start(path, speed, endaction, absolute) function inside a with statement (for the enemy the bullet collided with, of course, which, in this case, can only be the boss). The first argument is our path, (path_boss). The next is the speed at which it should move. For this, pass the number 6.

Our next parameter decides what to do once the path ends. They are as follows:

- 0: End path
- 1: Continue path from original point; jumps to start position if path is not closed
- 2: Continue from current position
- 3: Go backwards (reverse speed)

We'll use the second option (so pass 1). The final parameter takes a Boolean value, `true` for following the absolute path in the editor, `false` for following a relative path. Pass `true`, since we based our points on the room.

Outside the `if` that checked the boss' hp, put another `with` statement that has the boss object that we hit perform the **User Defined 0** event. The parameters you pass to the `event_perform` function will be `ev_other` and `ev_user0`, as User defined events are a type of **Other** event. So whenever the player's bullet hits the boss, the boss will increase the frequency with which it spawns missiles and enemies.

Now, we just have some code to add to the controller object we made, and then we're done with the boss! First, set the variable `steps` to 0 inside of the object's **Create** event. Next, inside of the **Alarm 0** event, find the `if` statement that checks whether an instance of the main ship exists. Have the `if` statement also require that an instance of the boss object doesn't exist and that the variable `steps` is less than 1800.

When that number of steps have passed, we will create the boss object. Now, add an `else if` clause that checks if the main ship and the boss object both exist. Inside, create two enemies at opposite ends of the screen (the boss will be created in the middle of the screen) so that there are more enemies other than those the boss pumps out.

When you're done with that event, add a **Step** event. Inside, increment the `steps` variable by 1. If it equals 1800, create an instance of the boss object in the middle of the screen.

Now, add the final event that we will need — a **Draw** event. Inside, set the color to draw with whatever you'd like, we chose dark gray. Then, we will use the `draw_set_halign(halign)` function, which chooses how to horizontally anchor what you draw. You might say it modifies the origin. By default, the coordinate you provide will be for the top-left corner of what you draw. But you can change it to the middle or by the right corner! The parameters you can pass are `fa_left`, `fa_center`, and `fa_right`, which are pretty self explanatory. We're going to anchor by the center, so choose `fa_center` as your argument to the function of course. The `draw_set_valign(valign)` function also exists, which takes `fa_top`, `fa_middle`, and `fa_bottom` as arguments.

Now, check if an instance of `class_enemy` doesn't exist and if the variable `steps` is more than `1800`. If so, draw a winning message at the center of the screen (by manipulating the height and width of the room). Otherwise, if an instance of the main ship does not exist, draw a losing message at the same position.

Congrats! You're done with the Boss AI, and you already have all the objects you need in the room. So you can test your game immediately. Do so, and make sure that the boss shows up after a minute, and that it randomly shoots missiles or enemies, and that after its `hp` is at `100`, it moves left and right. If that's all working, great job! You've only one more section to go through.

Particles

The final section of this chapter will introduce you to the use of particles in your game. Once you've gone through this, it should be child's play to use the extra functionality for them that we won't go over, since particles are very easy to set up and use, and they're also a very good component to get into the habit of using.

Before we begin coding particles, let's define what a particle is. A particle is a graphical resource defined by the particle type from which they are created, and they are displayed by using a particle system. They can create small or large effects without being CPU-intensive, allowing us to create cool effects without employing objects or sprites that could slow down the game. Particles create an organization for displaying your effects, and make it very easy. Particle types are "defined", so to speak, and are then displayed via a particle system directly, or through an emitter, which gives you some more functionality that you don't always need. We won't be using an emitter for the first particle we create in this chapter.

Let's create our first particle—an explosion particle. This chapter uses the project from the previous chapter, so you can simply modify that one or clone it. Once you've done either of the two, create an object called `obj_particle`. You can likely guess what we'll do in it. Add a **Create** event. Here, we will be setting up our particle system and types.

The first step is to create a particle system. It's generally good practice to have one particle system that you create at the start of the game and delete at the end (as they are dynamic resources, and cause a memory leak if they're not removed from memory), rather than creating a bunch of different systems, as that can get confusing and you'll take up way more resources than you have to. To create a particle system, assign a variable `global.ps` to the return value of the function `part_system_create()`. Skip a line or two, as now we will be creating two different particle types — a small and large explosion. The first will be for regular and missile enemies, whereas the second will be for the boss. Create a particle type by assigning `global.pt_explosion` to `part_type_create()`. Next, we specify the particle's shape with the function `part_type_shape(ind, shape)`. Pass it the index of the particle type to modify, which is stored in that variable we literally just created. Then, use the `pt_shape_explosion` shape as your second argument. Now, we can specify a size with `part_type_size(ind, size_min, size_max, size_incr, size_wiggle)`. Specify a minimum size of 0.25, a max of 0.3, an incrementation of 0.1, and a wiggle (how much should be randomly added/subtracted per step) of 0. The next function to be used is `part_type_color3(ind, color1, color2, color3)` so that we can give the particle three colors to move between. The `part_type_color1` (which takes one color) and `part_type_color2` particles (which takes two) also exist, but we're going to use three colors. The particle's color will fade from the first, to the second, to the third. The colors we will use are `c_orange`, `c_red` and `c_gray`, in that order. Our final function for this particle type is `part_type_life(ind, life_min, life_max)`. Give a minimum life of 30 steps, and a max of 60.

Nice job! You finished that particle type. Next, we will create another explosion. Since we already did the hard part, we will take what we did and adjust it for our next particle. Copy all the code for that particle type you already completed, and paste it below. Change all uses of `global.pt_explosion` to `global.pt_big_explosion` in this paste. Also, give it a minimum size of 2, a max of 5, and an incrementation of 0.5. Finally, give the new particle type a life of 60 to 90 steps rather than 30 to 60.

Congrats! You've made your particle system and its two types. However, particles are dynamic resources, so they *must* be removed when not needed. Add a **Game end** event to this object. Use `part_type_destroy(ind)` to destroy our two types, and `part_system_destroy(ind)` to destroy our system. You can now close out the object.

Let's now edit the `class_enemy` object. Give it a **Destroy** event. Inside, we will "spawn" particles using the function `part_particles_create(ind, x, y, parttype, number)`. We first pass our particle system, held in `global.ps`. Then, we pass the function the coordinates to spawn the particle at. (`x - (sprite_width / 2) - 8, y`) looked good to us. On the horizontal axis, this spawns it at the current x coordinate minus half of the width of the sprite the object is using minus 8. Our particle type will be chosen in the **Create** events of our enemies in a variable called `particle`, so pass `particle` for `parttype`. Then, since we only want one explosion to be created, pass 1 for the `number` parameter.

Now, close out that object, and we'll open up the enemy bullet object, for starters. Give it its own **Destroy** event, and put an **Execute Code** action in (the same one we've been using for everything since *Chapter 3, Introducing the GameMaker Language*). Put `///Parent Destroy Override` into it, and then close it out. So if you look at the **Destroy** event for this object, you'll see that comment without even opening the action (since if you remember, three forward slashes on the first line make the comment appear as the "title" or name of the **Action** in the drag and drop interface for GameMaker). From the previous chapter, recall that when a child object has an event, and its parent has that same event as well, the child doesn't run that event. Well, we don't want any particles associated with the enemy bullet, so we need to prevent it from running the event that would make it spawn particles, and so we've given it a nearly empty **Destroy** event.

We say nearly because we did put something in—a comment. Now, the thing about GameMaker is that it removes empty events from objects. So if you gave an object a **Draw** event but didn't put any code in it (maybe you're going to do that later), the workspace would actually delete the event from the object. You override this by just putting something into the event, in this case, a comment, but you could write `var foo = "bar"` if you wanted (but, of course, this takes some memory and uses the CPU when it doesn't need to), as that qualifies as putting something into the event.

So anyway, now that you've put in this **Destroy** event override, close out the object and open up the regular enemy object. Inside of its **Create** event, set the `particle` variable to `-1`. Next, we check if the particle `global.pt_explosion` exists using the `part_type_exists(ind)` function, as these enemies are spawned at the beginning of the game when the particle might not have been initialized. If the particle does exist, set `particle` to the global explosion particle. Close the **Create** event, and open the **Step** event. Check whether `particle` equals `-1` and if the explosion particle exists. Set `particle` to `global.pt_explosion`.

Now close out that event and the object, and put the *exact* same code in the missile object, except the new code in the **Step** event should go below the call to `event_inherited()`. Now, you can do the same thing for the boss object, but replace references to `global.pt_explosion` with `global.pt_big_explosion`.

Remember how we said that the enemies are created at the start of the game, but the particles might not be initialized yet? Well for that reason, we have to set the variable that the index of the regular explosion particle is held in to some value prior to the enemy setting its particle so that it doesn't reference a nonexistent variable. In order to do this, open the **Create** event of our control object. Set `global.pt_explosion` to `-1` at the top. In this way, the variable will exist for the enemy object when it references it, but it will still get the correct particle once the explosion particle has been initialized.

Great job! You've completed the work for the explosion particles, and can test your game. Ensure that all the particles function properly whenever you destroy an enemy or missile, and that after the boss is destroyed, the enemies are destroyed one by one, but not all at once. If it all works fine, move on!

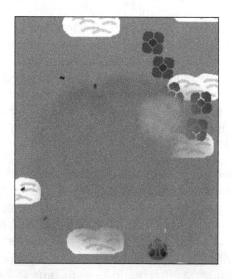

Now let's add a rain particle to our game via the use of a sprite and a particle emitter. Create a small raindrop sprite (around 8 x 8). Once you're satisfied with it, open up the `obj_particle` object's **Create** event. At the bottom, create a particle and hold its index in `pt_rain`. Now, rather than setting its shape, color, size, and other things, we simply set its sprite with `part_type_sprite(ind, sprite, animate, stretch, random)`. The first two parameters should be obvious, but as for the last three, they all take Boolean values for whether or not to follow the sprite's animation (`true` means yes, `false` means no), whether or not to stretch the animation to meet the particle's lifespan (true yes, false no), and whether or not to choose a random subimage (true yes, false no). Pass `false` for all three of those parameters. Next, let's give the particle a speed with `part_type_speed(ind, speed_min, speed_max, speed_incr, speed_wiggle)`. We found a minimum of 2, a max of 2.5, an incrementation of 0.2, and no wiggle looked best.

Following this, supply the particle a constant direction of down with `part_type_direction(ind, dir_min, dir_max, dir_incr, dir_wiggle)` by passing `270` for the minimum and maximum directions, and `0` for the incrementation and wiggle. After this, give the particle a lifespan of 300 steps.

Now that you have created your particle, find it in the **Create** event, where you created your particle system. Below this, create a particle emitter and hold its index in the `em` variable with `part_emitter_create(ps)`, and pass the function our particle system, held in `global.ps`. Now, since we're doing a rain particle, we'll specify a region for the emitter to "spawn" the rain particles using the function `part_emitter_region(ps, ind, xmin, xmax, ymin, ymax, shape, distribution)`. The first two parameters are the particle system that the emitter is in, followed by the emitter itself. Then we'll be passing the coordinates that specify the region. For this particle, we found that passing `0`, `room_width`, `-16`, and then `0` looked good. The particles will be created in this region, then move downwards. Following this, pass `ps_shape_rectangle` for a general rectangular distribution, and `ps_distr_linear` so that the particles have an equal chance of appearing anywhere, rather than being mostly created around the edges or center of the region.

Now you've finished setting up your emitter! We have only one more line of code for this **Create** event. When we tested the game like this, we noticed the rain did not appear on top of the boss object, rather it showed on top. In order to fix this, we can set the depth of our particle system. Right after you create the system, set its depth with `part_system_depth(ind, depth)`, giving it a depth of negative one million. Depth is relative, but for things that appear on top of everything, people generally give them extreme depths rather than something like `-10` so that they don't have to change it if they give something a depth of `-20`, for instance.

Now that you've finished the **Create** event, open up the **Game end** event for this object. **Destroy** our rain particle type, and then destroy the emitter with `part_emitter_destroy(ps, ind)`, passing it the system that the emitter is in, followed by the emitter. Now, let's actually spawn the particles. Add a **Step** event for this object. Inside, use `part_emitter_stream(ps, ind, parttype, number)`. Our type is of course the rain particle, and five looked nice to us. Once you've done all of this, you're done with your rain particle! So test your game, and make sure that the rain looks good and works perfectly.

The following is a screenshot of how it looked in our game:

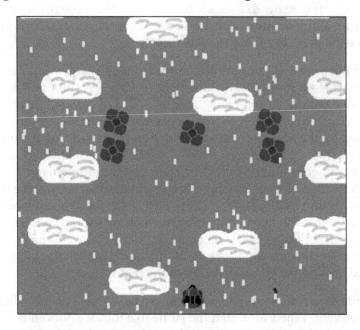

Summary

You learned a lot of different information in this chapter — parenting, how to create a tracking AI, change drawing alignment, creating your own events, creating and using paths, and implementing particles! Of course, go back and review the chapter to make sure you understand all the functions and everything else we taught you. In the following chapter, we will be overviewing the GameMaker physics engine and show you how to utilize its capabilities in two different ways — one of which you might not expect.

Review questions

1. What are **User defined** events for?

2. How do you make something move towards something else, but make sure not to hit what it isn't tracking?

3. How can you change the horizontal alignment (you might also call it the origin) from which text (and anything else) is drawn?

4. How do you set up parenting in GameMaker, and what is the purpose of setting up parent and child objects? What can you accomplish with the use of parent objects that you might not be able to otherwise?

5. Define and contrast particles, particle systems, and particle emitters.

6. How do you set up a particle with GameMaker's constants and with a sprite that you made?

7. What is the best practice for creating and using particle systems?

8. How did we stop the enemy bullet from having to use a particle?

9. What are objects (not in a GameMaker sense, but in terms of object-oriented programming)?

Quick drills

1. Add a score system to the game so that the player gets points as they play, and make the game endless.

2. Add a highscore display.

3. In line with the score system, create a system that has waves of increasing difficulty. Let the player know when they have reached the next wave.

4. Add a lives system for the main player (that is, start the game with three lives). In past games, you have created lives and displayed the lives using the main character sprite.

5. Give the player a speed powerup, as well as the ability to shoot a more powerful kind of bullet (which should of course require a longer recharge). Get creative and program another enemy AI. Look up some of the functions in the GameMaker documentation, while also using some of the ones that you've already learned to create a unique and challenging enemy.

6. Play around with your existing particle types so that they look how you want them to—particles are great for playing around with, as it's not like you can bug your game just by modifying some of their properties.

7. Create one or two new particle types, and play around with those as well.

8

Introducing the GameMaker: Studio Physics Engine

In this chapter, we will introduce the built-in GameMaker physics engine, based on the open source Box2D and LiquidFun physics engines. The engine has a lot of features that you might find beneficial, one of which being that you can create physics-based games. However, you are not restricted to using the engine for a sandbox style physics game. It has powerful and simple-to-use collision checking that can even be used for all the games we've made so far. You could refactor all of those games just by implementing physics! In this chapter, we'll program two small engines based on the physics engine in order to give you a small introduction into setting up the physics engine in your games.

A physics game

In this section, we will program a small physics sandbox. We're not going very in-depth, as this is intended to be a small introduction to the physics engine, not a complete tutorial. Let's first explain some information that you'll need to know when you're using GameMaker's physics engine. For one, you should not mix physics-specific code with code that controls movement that doesn't use physics (for example, use physics speed variables rather than the variable `speed`). It's also important to limit how many physics instances are active at once in your game, as they use intense calculations to make everything flow properly. In relation to this, use parenting for collision checks — children will not inherit physics properties, but they can inherit collision events. If you had five different enemies, it's best to have your player check for a collision with a parent rather than all five of those different enemies, if you can.

But anyway, let's start with making our physics game. The first step is to create the project, so do that. Then create two sprites—a ball sprite and a block sprite. Center their axis, but do nothing to their collision masks. The physics properties that we will set up will handle that.

Now create two objects, one for a ball and one for a block. We'll work with the block first. Assign the proper sprite, and then select the checkbox that says **Uses Physics**. Additional buttons and boxes will be made available to you to modify the physics properties of this object, but we only care about two of them. See the **Density** box? This controls the density of an object (well, of course), and thus controls its weight and how it is impacted by different forces and components of your physics world. However, we don't want our block to move at all. We want it to function as a wall and floor. In order to make an object "infinitely heavy", as one way to put it, set its density to 0.0. This will make it impossible to move.

Next, we will modify the collision shape (or fixture) of the object, so select the **Modify Collision Shape** button. A window will pop up for you to modify the points of the shape. By default, the shape you can have is a circle, but we choose the shape option (not a square, as when we put in code for the ball's collision with the block, it would fly straight up if it hit a side block). With the shape of the fixture that we will use, it will diagonally bounce, so select that one. The shape option allows you to create a nonconcavular polygonal collision shape with *n* sides. It will start as a triangle but you can add sides by adding points to the shape (keep it as a triangle for this though). Move the vertices of your triangle collision shape to have one in the top right, one in the top left, and then one 16 pixels below in the center. When you're done with that, close out that window, followed by the object's window:

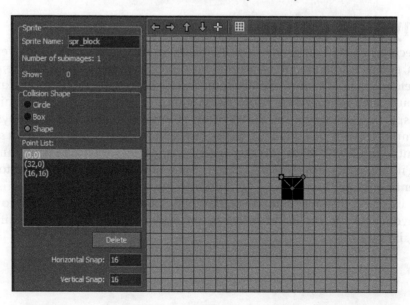

Now, we can work on the ball object. Give it a sprite and make it use physics, but go straight to modifying its collision shape — don't modify its density because we do want it to dynamically and actively interact with the physics of the game. Make the circle match up with the sprite, and then close out the collision shape window.

When using the GameMaker physics engine, in order to register a collision, we use the old drag and drop **Collision** event; we don't use the collision functions. So whenever you're using the GameMaker physics engine, make sure to use the **Collision** event if you want a collision registered between two objects; otherwise, they'll pass right through each other. So right now, add to the ball object a **Collision** event with the block object. Inside, we will apply force to the ball with the function `physics_apply_force(x, y, xforce, yforce)`. The forces are measured in Newtons. We want the ball to "bounce", so apply an `xforce` of 0 and a `yforce` of `-5000` at (x, y).

Now let's add another **Collision** event to this object — with another instance of the ball object. Inside, use the same function we just used with all the same arguments except for `yforce`. Rather than `-5000`, pass `-1000 * (other.y - (other.sprite_height / 2) - y)`. This will give an upward motion of 1000 Newtons multiplied by the difference between the y coordinate bottom of the ball on top and the y coordinate of the center of the bottom ball, so that the top ball will go up and the bottom one will go down. When you play the game, you'll see what we mean.

The final object we'll make is `obj_control`. In its **Step** event, put a `if` statement. We will check whether the player has clicked the left mouse button by using the function `mouse_check_button_pressed(button)`. Pass it to `mb_left` for the left mouse button.

Inside the `if` statement, put another `if` statement that checks whether `instance_count` (which tells you how many instances are active in the room) is higher than 200. We don't want to have too many balls (which would be physics instances) active in the room at once (clicking will be creating these after we put in that code soon).

Inside of that `if` statement, insert a `for` loop. Set the local variable `i` to 0, check whether it is less than `instance_count`, and then increment our counter. In each iteration of our loop, check whether the coordinates of the instance whose ID is held in `instance_id[i]` (an array of the IDs of all active instances in the room) are outside the room. However, rather than checking whether their y coordinate is less than 0 in one of the conditions, check if it is less than `-32` so that we don't delete instances close to the game screen (in this way, we can be sure to make it seem as though no balls are randomly being lost). Only the ball objects could possibly be outside of the room, so we needn't check whether the instance is one of the ball objects.

If that `if` statement returned `true`, then destroy the instance whose `id` is in `instance_id[i]`. Then break out of the `for` loop (with `break` of course). Outside the `if` statement, we checked whether the count of active instances was higher than `200`, create an instance of the ball object at `(mouse_x, mouse_y)` so that one will spawn at the mouse cursor's position.

Now close out that object, and make a new room. In the **physics** tab, check the **Room is Physics World** box, and then proceed to put in your control object and blocks as walls and a floor. Don't put in a ceiling. Once you've finished that, compile and run your game, and you should be able to create balls by clicking anywhere on the screen and see them bouncing off of the blocks and other balls.

So this game doesn't really have a lot going on yet, and there's an important physics feature we haven't showed you yet—joints! These are what allow you to bind physics instances together at a certain point in order to have them behave in certain ways (you might want a motor, or a car!). What we'll be creating is a platform joint to a base on the floor. When the balls bounce on it, it will rotate. If it goes fast enough, then it can apply force to other balls that hit it. This is actually pretty easy to set up.

Begin with creating two sprites—a rectangle and a triangle. Center the rectangle sprite's origin. As for the triangle sprite, only center it on the *x* axis, but have the *y* coordinate of its origin be `0` (at the top).

Now create two objects for each of those two sprites. Give the rectangle a collision shape that matches its sprite completely, and then open up the triangle object. Give this one a density of `0.0` (so it doesn't move and doesn't fall through the floor), and then give it a triangular collision shape.

Now, inside this object's **Create** event, we'll joint the rectangle and the triangle with a revolute joint. This allows one instance to revolve around the other with a certain degree of freedom. Use the function `physics_joint_revolute_create(inst1, inst2, w_anchor_x, w_anchor_y, ang_min_limit, ang_max_limit, ang_limit, max_motor_torque, motor_speed, motor, col)`. It's a long function, but we'll go through its arguments step by step.

The first two arguments are the two instances to join. These will be `id` and `obj_rectangle`. `id` is the instance ID of the triangle object, which is calling this function. Then pass the `x` and `y` coordinates of the triangle object. Following this, pass two zeros, and then a `false`, and then two more zeros, and another `false`. We will not limit the angle of this joint to a minimum nor a maximum, nor will we use a motor (which would force a revolution to always occur). Then, pass `false` for the last argument, since we don't want our two instances to register collisions, nor do we really care about them actually. We just want the rectangle to revolve freely about the tip of the triangle.

Once you've done all of that, open up the ball object, and give it a **Collision** event with the rectangle object. Make sure to put in an empty **Execute Code** block with a comment so that the event is not deleted.

When you're done setting up collisions and joints and other physics related properties, place the triangle object on the "floor" of the room, and then put the rectangle directly above it. Then test your game as usual:

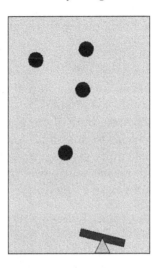

A final note before we move onto the next game—when you're deactivating instances in a game using physics, make sure to set `phy_active` to `false` for all the instances using physics (and then `true` when reactivating).

The physics engine in a regular game

The remainder of this chapter will be a small tutorial on how to incorporate physics into a top-down style game, like our first one. We're just going to create a small engine to demonstrate how you would move around a player and get perfect collisions.

So first create a simple player sprite and wall sprite. They can be simple squares or complex shapes if you want. Make sure that you center the origins—it's important for the collisions to work properly.

Now create a player and wall object. Give the wall its sprite, a density of `0`, and a collision shape. If you made the sprite complex (although walls are usually blocky), then select the **Shape** option and plot a series of points to get a collision shape that matches the wall and then open up the player object. Give the player its sprite and a collision shape. If the player's sprite is complex, then use the **Shape** option.

Now let's make the player move and stop at the wall. Add a **Create** event, and set `phy_fixed_rotation` to `true`. If we left this in its default state (`false`), then when pushing against a wall, the player would rotate slightly, but we don't want that, we want it to look like it's in a normal top-down game.

After this, set `hspd` and `vspd` to `0`. Add a **Step** event to the object. If the player is pressing the left arrow key, set our horizontal speed to `-5`. If they're pressing the right arrow key, then set it to positive `5`. And if we're pressing both or neither of the keys, set our horizontal speed to `0`. Following this, put in the same code but for the up and down arrow keys.

Once you've done this, we'll actually modify the coordinates of the player. No longer can you use `x` and `y` however, instead you will use `phy_position_x` and `phy_position_y`. Increment both these variables by our horizontal and vertical speeds, respectively of course. Then set both of our speeds to `0`. Once you've completed this, add a **Collision** event to this object for when it hits the wall. Recall how we said GameMaker deletes empty events. As such, you'll need to add a comment to the event so that it has *some* "substance" to it and so that a collision is registered, but without anything extra being done.

Once you've finished, make a new room. Make it a physics world under the physics tab. Also under that tab, set the **Y Gravity** to `0` so that nothing is pulled downwards. Then put in walls and the player object, and run your game. See how perfect the collisions are and how the movement is still perfect? And it was so easy to implement, right? The physics engine is pretty great!

Summary

Kudos on finishing this introductory physics chapter! The following, and final, chapter will wrap this up, and include debugging and some other useful information that we couldn't teach you as of yet.

Review questions

1. What is a fixture?
2. What is a joint?
3. How can you give a physics object "infinite weight"?
4. What variables do we use for the coordinates of an object that uses physics?
5. How can you check whether a mouse button is clicked, and how can you check the cursor's position?

Quick drills

1. Play around with different shapes in your sandbox game and see how they all interact. Have one of your shapes spawn when the player clicks the right mouse button (`mb_right`).

2. Also play around with revolution joints, maybe have balls that collide revolute. If you want, you could try some of the other joint types shown in GameMaker's documentation to see how they work.

3. In your second game, add a projectile that the player can spawn that uses physics properties. Program it just like the ones in previous games.

9
Wrapping Up

This final chapter will cover a variety of important information that is rather useful but did not find its way into the earlier chapters. The main section is on debugging, but we've included additional information. You won't be programming anything until the *Quick drills* section, and those won't be actual games—you'll be causing errors on purpose.

So without further ado, let's begin the chapter!

Debugging

You will learn about some of GameMaker's debugging capabilities. Before that, we'd like to show you a lightweight debugger console that you can modify and add to any game project to help with the debugging process. We've used it before, and it has been very helpful. Find it at `http://gmc.yoyogames.com/index.php?showtopic=675236`.

As for regular debugging, GameMaker: Studio has four features for debugging:

- Compile-time errors
- Runtime errors
- Debugger module
- Debugging functions

Compile-time errors are probably the easiest to fix, since they directly tell you what the issue is. Runtime errors still tell you the issue, but the runner is unable to know exactly what is causing the issue. Furthermore, a runtime error might not always occur, so you'll have to test your game many different times with many different conditions in order to eliminate all the bugs that you can. As far as the debugger, it's rather similar to any other debugger for a compiled program; it just has some GameMaker specific features. Finally, GameMaker has some debugging-specific functions (some of which you know of already, such as `show_message`). Now we will explain each of these features in detail.

Compile-time errors

We'll first go a little bit in-depth with compile-time errors. Again, note that you won't need to write any code for this chapter yet, so just read along.

We've created an object called `obj_foo`, and in its **Create** event, we've had it call `scr_foo()`. We put it in a room, and then got the following compile-time error when we attempted to run the game:

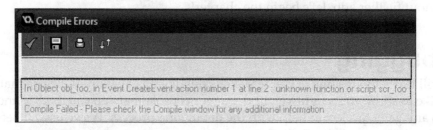

Now before you even saw the preceding image, you should have known what was wrong—we never created a `scr_foo`. However, now you know what a compile-time error would look like. It tells us the object we had an error in, the event, the action, the line number (actually, we wrote the call on **line 1**, so when you get these errors, look in the general vicinity of the line it tells you where the error occurred), and what the error was (in this case, `scr_foo` isn't a script or function).

There are a variety of compile-time errors that you can get, and they are generally easy to understand and they help the programmer locate and fix the error. One error might be that you attempted to set a read-only variable to some value. If you did that, the **Compile Errors** window would tell you all the same information as it did in the error shown previously, except the error itself would be different. Every error message follows the same format.

Runtime errors

The next error we will show you is a runtime error. These are still easy to fix (at least most of the time), but new users to GameMaker often get confused by the large bulk of messages that the runner tells you. Usually, you'll only end up using one small part of the error message, so it's important to know where to look. But by the end of this section, you'll know how to find your way around a runtime error.

In order to create a runtime error, we've put the following code in the **Create** event of `obj_foo` (and we have of removed the call to `scr_foo`):

```
for (var i = 0; i < 3; ++i) foo[i] = i;
var a = foo[3];
```

Right away, you should see the issue; we've attempted to reference the nonexistent fourth position in the array called `foo`. When we run the game, we get the following error:

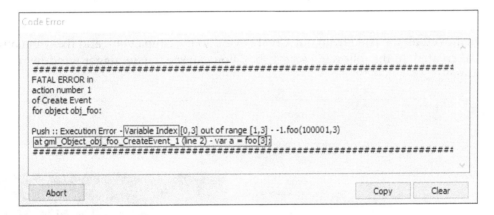

So in this screenshot, you see a lot of words and information in the error message. Since you already know what the error is, you might be able to decipher the important information from this error, but let's explain parts of the message that you need, which we've boxed. We first see that this is a **Variable Index** error. Array indexes are nothing more than variable pointers, so here the error is with a variable index not existing.

Following this is the really important part that you need; it tells you exactly where the error occurred, and you can even see the code from that line in the window.

The most common error that people get is a **Variable Get** error, where they attempt to access a variable that doesn't exist. This is because, while we all try to be perfect, nobody is that great at typing or remembering the names they gave their variables. For instance, you might declare a variable called a, and then reference A. Or perhaps, you'll declare a variable called socket, and reference sockets. There is a variety of errors that the GameMaker runner will spit out, but now you should know how to decipher them.

The GameMaker: Studio debugger

In this next section, we will overview the use of the GameMaker: Studio debugger, which is likely the most important feature of GameMaker's four debugging features, as this allows you to see how your code is running and working while the program is running. Like in any other debugger, you can set breakpoints; see local and global variable values; step into, over, and out of code; and there are also features to the debugger that are tailored for use with GameMaker. Without further ado, let's show it to you!

We've moved all the code from our **Create** event to the **Step** event, and fixed the bug we had created. In the following screenshot, you can see the debugger window for the game:

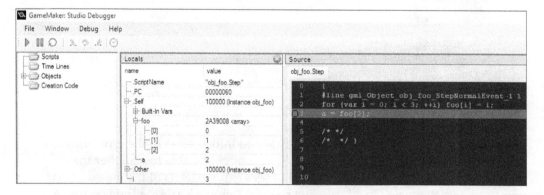

We've set a breakpoint by double-clicking on line 3 in the debugger, so in the **Locals** pane, we can see the contents of the foo array and the values of the variables a and i (the latter of which shows up in **Other** because it is a local variable). To open up new panes, right-click a pane's name, select **Set Type**, and choose the desired type (of which there are a lot, all helpful). The helpful ones are the **Source** (especially), **Locals**, and **Globals** variables, and **All Instances** (showing you variables of different instances of objects in your game).

If you want two panes open, right-click on a pane's name, select **Split**, and then choose the desired split direction. A new pane called **Empty** will be created, and then just choose that one's type.

In the top bar, the green play button resumes the game (puts in on top of the debugger window, and resumes it if it is stopped). The green pause button stops the game, and the circular arrow resets it. Following this, your yellow arrows are **Step In**, **Step Over**, and **Step Out** (for when going through the code step by step - going into a script, running the script without entering it, and going out of a script and into the main code). Then, the clock is for real-time updates, which doesn't always work in every case (so instead, we usually just set breakpoints and check values then).

Along the left side is where you can access different code blocks (scripts and events, the latter of which is under each object in the **Objects** folder). Double-click on one to see the source and set breakpoints. The GameMaker debugger is very easy to use and is very beneficial to the debugging process, as with any debugger.

Debugging functions

The final feature that GameMaker has available to use for the debugging process is a set of debugging-specific functions and variables. The following is a table of what is available to use:

Code	Description
`debug_mode`	`true` when running a game in the debug mode, and `false`, when in regular mode.
`get_integer(str, def)`	This opens a prompt for you to enter an integer. Pass it a prompt message and default value.
`get_string(str, def)`	This opens a prompt for you to enter a string. Parameters are the same as `get_integer`.
`show_error(str, abort)`	This shows a specific error message. Pass `true` for the second argument to abort the game, and `false` to continue as usual.
`show_message(str)`	This shows a message.
`show_question(str)`	This asks a yes/no question. It returns `true`/`false` for yes/no.
`show_debug_message(string)`	This shows a debug message in the compile window (not a pop up).

Code	Description
`show_debug_overlay(enable)`	This shows important debugging information: I/O processing, step event speed, draw event time, debug update time, time waiting for GPU to finish drawing a frame, text render time, screen clearing time, and GPU flush. Pass `true` to enable it, `false` to disable it.
`code_is_compiled()`	This checks whether the code was compiled with the YoYo Compiler properly.
`fps`	This returns how many CPU steps GameMaker is actually completing — limit of your room speed.
`fps_real`	This returns the actual number of CPU steps GameMaker is actually completing (not limited by the room speed).

We'll now use a few of these functions in tandem. We put a **Create** event back into our object and put the following code into it:

```
if (debug_mode) {
    show_debug_overlay(true);
    show_debug_message("DEBUG MESSAGE");
    show_message("DEBUG MESSAGE");
}
```

The following is a screenshot of the game being run with the compile window alongside it:

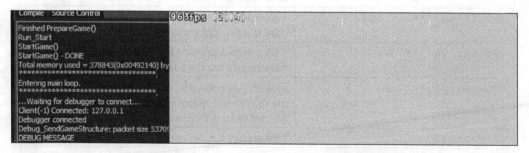

You can't see the regular `show_message` call, since we felt showing the overlay was more important, and the overlay is rendered (so it comes after the **Create** event). You already know what `show_message` looks like though, you've used it. At the bottom of the compile window is the output of our call to `show_debug_message`. In the game window, you can see the debug overlay (somewhat, the game doesn't really take up a lot of resources).

Helpful information on GameMaker

This section is sort of a "mash-up" of a bunch of important information that we didn't get to tell you before, but that we will now. Some of it is especially helpful to prevent you from writing code that would be flawless in other languages but incorrect in GML.

Before we begin though, a very useful GameMaker community is located at `https://www.reddit.com/r/gamemaker` (and we've linked another later). The community is very helpful and answers any questions you might have, and they sometimes post projects and code that you can use that might be tedious to make otherwise. The same goes for the community linked later.

Quirks of the GameMaker Language

So the first bit of information will be on the GameMaker Language. Let's talk about data types. Pretty simple, right? They include `int`, `float`, `double`, `char`, `string`, and `bool`. Well, GameMaker actually only has `float` and `string`. Integers are just real numbers, and characters are just strings. There are no Booleans. `true` and `false` are actually constants, and values that count as `true` are `0.5` and above, and ones that count as `false` are below `0.5`. It's important to know this in case you write code that relies on -1 being `true` rather than `false` (and rightfully so, as other programming languages count 0 as the only `false` value) and then it doesn't work.

Another GameMaker quirk: = is the same as == when it comes to conditions. While there is the advantage of not having to worry about forgetting to type the second equal sign, there is the disadvantage that you lose the ability to write assignments in your conditions like you would be able to do in other languages such as C++. It's not a big flaw (you can still put your assignments elsewhere and have the code work the same), but now you won't attempt this and, as such, won't cause a **Variable Get** error to occur when your code would seem perfectly fine.

A final, and very useful tip, is that if you ever find yourself limited by GameMaker's features, you can find extensions that expand upon GameMaker's ability on the GameMaker forums (`http://gmc.yoyogames.com`) and on the GameMaker Marketplace (`https://marketplace.yoyogames.com`). People program these extensions to put extra functions into their projects so that they aren't limited by what GameMaker can do. Furthermore, if you ever find yourself stuck and can't figure out how to program something, chances are that part of what you need or something related might be available in either of the two aforementioned places, or in the Reddit link provided previously.

Unexplained resources

You've likely noticed that there are some resources in GameMaker that we haven't even touched. These include:

- **Shaders**: These are small programs that run on the GPU and modify each pixel on your screen. These however, are not written in GML, rather, they are written in the **OpenGL ES Shading Language**, which is very syntactically different from GML (the shader language is far closer to the C language). Given their complexity and high contrast from GML, we did not go over them.

- **Timelines**: These allow you to specify exactly what will happen at different steps in your game. This makes it easy to set up routines for your objects to follow at different times in your game. Timelines have their own special editor; however, you will find parts of it very similar to the regular object editor.

- **Macros**: These are also known as constants. These are very easy to use. If you don't know what a macro, or a constant, is, it's a variable with a value that cannot change. You typically give your macros names in uppercase, and they are commonly used for colors that you create with functions such as `make_color_rgb(red, green, blue)`. Your colors will be constant, of course, so it's easiest to have them as macros. Sometimes, macros are also used for version numbers, company names, game names, or for other information.

Furthermore, if you are using the Professional Edition of GameMaker, you might have noticed the **Configuration** section on the top bar. These let you specify different options for each platform (explained next) that you export to. In relation to macros, every configuration gets its own set of macros alongside the global macros you might see labeled as **All Configurations**.

Export modules

So GameMaker has different export modules (or "targets" or "platforms", as they are sometimes called), which are just different operating systems and hardware that you can publish your game to. All of them have some differences (except for desktop—you don't really need to worry about incompatibilities and such with those except for a few Windows-specific functions that you likely won't use anyway).

However, for the others, there are things you'll need to learn via the docs that weren't taught in this book (such as touch controls on mobile or the Steam API) simply since we can't assume that you even have the Professional Edition of GameMaker: Studio in this book, and Windows/desktop is the easiest to start learning with, since it's the export already available to you and you don't have to set up compiling and debugging over your LAN. The Standard version of GameMaker: Studio is free and allows you to publish to a windows executable or self-extracting installer. The other modules can be purchased separately (assuming you have the Professional Edition of GameMaker) or as part of the GameMaker: Studio Master Collection. This will be required if you would like to publish your games to iOS, Android, Mac, or other platforms.

Some of the modules also don't support some functions (HTML5 doesn't work with binary files nor networking).

Summary

Congratulations! You've finished this entire book and can now begin your life as a game developer, or a hobbyist game developer (or perhaps continue and learn different game development engines). You learned a lot of information throughout the course of this book—from input, to drawing, to menus, to networking, to the file system, to particles, and a whole lot more! Quite a lot of code! Now if you're ever confused about something or forgot something, the answer is probably right in this book for you to quickly reference. In addition to using the book as a reference you should now be comfortable using the resources provided in GameMaker: Studio as well as the online GameMaker community.

Review questions

1. What are the different features available for debugging in GameMaker: Studio?

2. What is the difference between compile-time and runtime errors?

3. What is the purpose of a timeline?

4. What are shaders?

Quick drills

1. Purposefully, create bugs in a project that would give compile-time and runtime errors and see what GameMaker tells you about them.

2. Visit the GameMaker Community (`http://gmc.yoyogames.com/`) and become a member of the forums. At this point, you should be able to assist others with issues they might have with GML and GameMaker: Studio, as well as be assisted by the people in the community!

3. Here is some flawed code; figure out where the problems are:

```
5 = foo;
--------
foo = 1;
bar = foobar;
-------------
While(true) {}
-------------
for (var i = 0; i < 10; ++i) foo[i] = 0;
bar = foo[10];
-------------------------------------------
foo = "bar;
```

Index

Symbols

2D arrays
using, in programming 84-89

A

ASCIITable
URL 102
Aseprite
about 118
URL 118
aspect ratio 21
Asynchronous Networking event
about 132
connection, handling 133
data, handling 134-136
disconnection, handling 133, 134

B

backgrounds 38, 39
basic collision checking 27
Boss AI
programming 157-161
buffer 126

C

client
in client/server system 137-142
client/server multiplayer networking
about 126
actual server, creating 130, 131
IP address, printing of server on
screen 127-130
port, printing of server on screen 127-130

client/server networking 127
collision mask 27
compile-time errors 178
constants 184
controller object 31
customizable controls
about 109-113
control configurations, saving 114

D

datagram 126
data structure (DS) 95
debugger 5
debugging 177
debugging console engine
reference link 177
debugging, features
compile-time errors 178
debugger 180, 181
functions 181, 182
runtime errors 179
debugging functions 181, 182
depth 12
documentation, GameMaker: Studio
about 6
reference link 6

E

endless platformer
creating 77, 78
death, incorporating into game 81, 82
enemies, incorporating into game 81, 82
menus, implementing 90-94
player, bouncing 78-80

player movement 78-80
random spawning 83
textboxes, implementing 95-97
enemies, Escape the Dungeon game
about 28
moving 28-30
player, damaging 30-34
Escape the Dungeon game
creating 19
enemies 28
keys and locks, advancing to next
room 40, 41
playable character 20
walls 26, 27
working on enemy's shooting
mechanics 36-38
working on player's shooting
mechanics 34-36
Escape the Dungeon game, in GML
about 46
collisions 57
enemies, coding 58-62
events 49-51
health system 64-66
health variables, displaying 66-69
invincibility 69, 70
key objects, creating 74
lives system 64-66
lives variables, displaying 66-69
lock objects, creating 74
player, moving 53-56
player object, coding 51-53
player object, remaking 49
random seeds, creating 62-64
scripts 74
shooting capabilities 71, 72
sounds 73
sprites, remaking 46-49
subimage, modifying 56, 57
example project
about 6
coordinate planes 12
game, testing 14, 15
naming convention 6, 7
object, creating 10, 11
room, creating 13
sprite, drawing 8, 9

explosion particle
creating 161
export modules 184, 185

G

game 1
GameMaker
resources 184
GameMaker community
reference link 183
GameMaker forums
reference link 183
GameMaker Language
quirks 183
GameMaker Language (GML) 1
GameMaker Marketplace
reference link 183
GameMaker: Player 3
GameMaker: Studio
about 2
benefits 2
documentation 6
interface 4, 5
reference link, for licenses 3
version, selecting 3
GameMaker: Studio debugger 180, 181
**GameMaker: Studio, for Microsoft
Windows**
download link 3
Games Showcase, YoYo Games
reference link 2
Guxt
URL 149

H

highscore
loading 104-107
saving 104-107

I

INI file encryption 107-109
INI (initialization) 104
**Integrated Development
Environment (IDE) 2**
interface, GameMaker: Studio 4, 5

Internet Assigned Numbers Authority
   (IANA) 127
IP address 126
IP address, of server
   printing, on screen 127-130

J

JoyToKey
   URL 142

K

keyboard ghosting
   about 71
   reference link 71
key-related events
   differences 23

L

legacy gamepad support 143, 144
licenses, GameMaker: Studio
   reference link 3

M

macros 184
modern gamepad support 145
movement
   programming 120-122

N

networking terminology
   buffer 126
   client/server networking 127
   datagram 126
   IP address 126
   packet 126
   port 127
   socket 126
   Transmission Control Protocol (TCP) 126
   User Datagram Protocol (UDP) 126

O

OpenGL ES Shading Language 184

P

packet 126
particle emitter
   setting up 164, 165
particles
   about 161
   creating 161-164
physics engine, in regular game 173
physics game 169-173
playable character, Escape the
      Dungeon game
   about 20
   object 23-26
   sprite, creating 20-22
port 127
port, of server
   printing, on screen 127-130
precise collision checking 27

R

random spawning 83
resources, GameMaker
   macros 184
   shaders 184
   timelines 184
room speed 13
runtime errors 179

S

scoring system
   about 101-104
   highscore, loading 104-107
   highscore, saving 104-107
scrolling platformer
   making scroll 123-125
scrolling shooter game
   Boss AI, programming 157-160
   enemies, creating 151
   main ship, creating 149-151
   parenting, in objects 151-156
   random enemy spawning 156, 157
shaders 184
socket 126
sounds 39, 40

sprytefont 102
sprites
  animating 117-119
  creating 20-22
spritesheet
  importing 119, 120
subimage 8

T

timelines 184
Transmission Control Protocol (TCP) 126

U

User Datagram Protocol (UDP) 126
User Interface (UI) 2

V

version, GameMaker: Studio
  selecting 3
virtual key 54

W

walls, Escape the Dungeon game 26, 27
Wireshark
  URL 142

X

Xbox gamepad support
  integrating 142, 143
  legacy gamepad support 143, 144
  modern gamepad support 145
Xpadder
  URL 142

Y

YoYo Games
  reference link, for guide 15

Z

zero-based indexing 9

Thank you for buying
GameMaker Programming By Example

About Packt Publishing

Packt, pronounced 'packed', published its first book, *Mastering phpMyAdmin for Effective MySQL Management*, in April 2004, and subsequently continued to specialize in publishing highly focused books on specific technologies and solutions.

Our books and publications share the experiences of your fellow IT professionals in adapting and customizing today's systems, applications, and frameworks. Our solution-based books give you the knowledge and power to customize the software and technologies you're using to get the job done. Packt books are more specific and less general than the IT books you have seen in the past. Our unique business model allows us to bring you more focused information, giving you more of what you need to know, and less of what you don't.

Packt is a modern yet unique publishing company that focuses on producing quality, cutting-edge books for communities of developers, administrators, and newbies alike. For more information, please visit our website at www.packtpub.com.

Writing for Packt

We welcome all inquiries from people who are interested in authoring. Book proposals should be sent to author@packtpub.com. If your book idea is still at an early stage and you would like to discuss it first before writing a formal book proposal, then please contact us; one of our commissioning editors will get in touch with you.

We're not just looking for published authors; if you have strong technical skills but no writing experience, our experienced editors can help you develop a writing career, or simply get some additional reward for your expertise.

PUBLISHING

GameMaker Game
Programming with GML

Learn GameMaker Language programming concepts and
script integration with GameMaker: Studio through hands-on,
playable examples

Matthew DeLucas   PACKT

GameMaker Game Programming with GML

ISBN: 978-1-78355-944-2   Paperback: 350 pages

Learn GameMaker Language programming concepts
and script integration with GameMaker: Studio
through hands-on, playable examples

1. Write and utilize scripts to help organize and
   speed up your game production workflow.

2. Display important user interface components
   such as score, health, and lives.

3. Play sound effects and music, and create
   particle effects to add some spice to your
   projects.

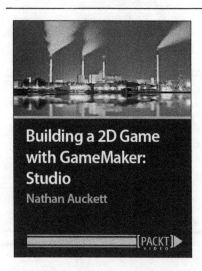

Building a 2D Game
with GameMaker:
Studio

Nathan Auckett

[PACKT]
VIDEO

Building a 2D Game with GameMaker: Studio [Video]

ISBN: 978-1-78355-876-6   Duration: 02:13 hours

All you need to know to get started with GameMaker:
Studio

1. Learn how to use GameMaker: Studio and
   its interface.

2. Program in Game Maker Language (GML).

3. Create your very own artificial intelligence.

Please check **www.PacktPub.com** for information on our titles

Android 5 Programming by Example

ISBN: 978-1-78528-844-9   Paperback: 212 pages

Turn your ideas into elegant and powerful mobile applications using the latest Android Studio for the Android Lollipop platform

1. Design and customize GUI using material design to create attractive and intuitive layouts easily.

2. Bring your designs to life with Android 5's powerful and extensive Java libraries, new sensors, and new platforms such as TVs, wearables, and cars.

3. An example-based guide to learn and develop applications for Android 5.

HTML5 Game Development with GameMaker

ISBN: 978-1-84969-410-0   Paperback: 364 pages

Experience a captivating journey that will take you from creating a full-on shoot 'em up to your first social web browser game

1. Build browser-based games and share them with the world.

2. Master the GameMaker Language with easy to follow examples.

3. Every game comes with original art and audio, including additional assets to build upon each lesson.

Please check **www.PacktPub.com** for information on our titles

9781785887963